THE MUSIC BOOK

Eunice Boardman
Professor of Music Education
University of Wisconsin
Madison, Wisconsin

Barbara Andress
Professor of Music Education
Arizona State University
Tempe, Arizona

Music Consultant
Buryl Red
Composer, Arranger, and Conductor

Special Consultants

Mervin W. Britton
Professor of Music
Arizona State University
Tempe, Arizona

Beth Landis
Former Director of Music Education
City Schools
Riverside, California

Betty Welsbacher
Director, Special Music Education
Wichita State University
Wichita, Kansas

Consultants

Martha Mahoney
Elementary Music Department Head
Elementary Schools
Milford, Connecticut

Keith Thompson
Associate Professor, Music Education
Pennsylvania State University
University Park, Pennsylvania

Donald Regier
Supervisor of Vocal Music
Secondary Schools
Baltimore County, Maryland

Nelmatilda Woodard
Director, Bureau of Music Education
Board of Education
City of Chicago

Holt, Rinehart and Winston, Publishers
New York, Toronto, London, Sydney

Consultants

Portions of this book previously published in Exploring Music 🎵

Copyright © 1975, 1971, 1966 by Holt, Rinehart and Winston

Copyright © 1981 by Holt, Rinehart and Winston, Publishers
All rights reserved
Printed in the United States of America

ISBN: 0-03-042216-7

12345   071   9876543

ACKNOWLEDGMENTS

Grateful acknowledgment is given to the following authors and publishers.

Appleseed Music, Inc., for "The Power and Glory," Copyright © 1963.
For "We Live at the Edge of Town," English text by Ruth Rubin. Used by permission.

Berandol Music Limited, for "Ancient Dance" ("Canarie"), from *Basic Recorder Technique,* edited by Hugh Orr. Used by permission.

Boosey and Hawkes, Inc., for "Old Abram Brown." Used by permission.

W. C. Brown Publications, for "The Alley Cat," from *Folk Dancing for Students and Teachers* by Mynatt and Kalman. Used by permission.

Chappell Music Company for "Who's Gonna Shoe Your Pretty Little Foot?" Found in *Folksong Encyclopedia,* Vol. 1, copyright © 1975 by Chapell & Co., Inc. This arrangement © 1980 by Chappell Co., Inc. International copyright secured. All rights reserved. Used by permission.

Colgems-EMI Music, Inc., for "You've Got a Friend." Used by permission.

Consolidated Music Publishers, for "The Blues Ain't Nothin'," from *The Blues Bag* by Happy Traum. Used by permission.

J. Curwen & Sons, Limited for "Allelujah." English translation by W. H. Draper from *School Worship.* Used by permission.

Fideree Music Co., for "As the Sun Goes Down." Used by permission.

Generic Music for "Down by the Riverside." Copyright © 1971, Generic Music. For arrangements of "Greensleeves," "Bound for the Promised Land," and "He's Got the Whole World in His Hands." Copyright © 1975, Generic Music. Used by permission.

Gypsy Boy Music, Inc., for "Groundhog," as adapted by Buffe Ste. Marie. Used by permission.

Hollis Music, Inc., for "Consider Yourself." Used by permission.

Frank Loesser, for "Wonderful Copenhagen." Used by permission.

Ludlow Music, Inc., for "Gonna Build a Mountain," "Roll on, Columbia," "Trinidad," and "Why, Oh Why?" Used by permission.

Macmillan Publishing Co., Inc., for "Swift Things Are Beautiful," from *Away Goes Sally* by Elizabeth Coatsworth. Copyright 1934 by Macmillan Publishing Co., Inc., © renewed 1962 by Elizabeth Coatsworth Beston. Used by permission.

Mills Music, Inc., for "Tzena, Tzena." Used by permission.

Northern Songs, Ltd., for "Blackbird." Used by permission.

Jack Owens, for "The Hukilau Song." Used by permission.

Oxford University Press, for "Ev'ry Night When the Sun Goes In." From *Folksongs from the Southern Appalachians,* copyright 1917 by the Oxford University Press. Used by permission.

Peer International Corporation, for "Sunny Day," and for "The Cage." Used by permission.

Prophet Music, Inc., for "Song Sung Blue." Used by permission.

E. C. Schirmer Music Company, for "The Silver Moon Is Shining." Used by permission.

G. Schirmer, Inc., for "Manomolela," from *Choral Folksongs of the Nabtu* by Williams & Maselwa. English lyrics by Pete Seeger, copyright © 1960 by G. Schirmer, Inc. Used by permission.

CONTENTS

Unit I
LEARN BY HEARING

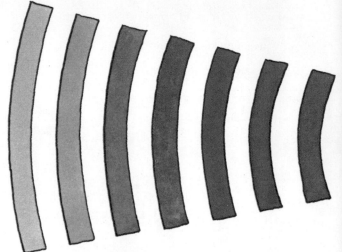

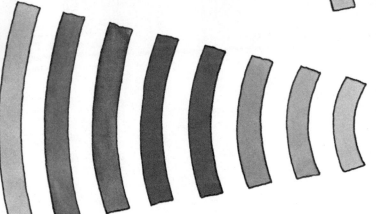

THE INDEPENDENT MUSICIAN

Which of these can you now do independently?			
learn words and melodies by hearing	learn harmonies to play and sing by hearing	identify musical elements	express your own musical ideas
In which areas will you commit yourself to becoming more independent?			

A musician can learn to perform new music by LISTENING or by LOOKING.
Which way will you learn "Gonna Build a Mountain"?

GONNA BUILD A MOUNTAIN

Words and Music by
Leslie Bricusse and Anthony Newley

Gon-na build a moun-tain_ Yeah, yeah   from a lit-tle

hill.   Yeah, yeah   Gon-na build a   moun-tain_ Yeah, yeah

least I hope I   will. Yeah, yeah   Gon-na build a

moun-tain_Yeah, yeah   Gon-na build it   high. Yeah, yeah   I don't know

how I'm gon-na do it,   on-ly know I'm gon-na   try. Yeah, yeah

From the musical production "Stop The World—I Wanna Get Off."
Words & Music by Leslie Bricusse & Anthony Newley.

1

WALKIN' IN THE SUNSHINE

Words and Music by Roger Miller

Some musicians learn music by listening to other people perform and repeating what they have heard.

Learn the songs on the following pages in this way.

Walkin' in the sunshine, sing a little sunshine song,
Put a smile upon your face as if there's nothin' wrong.
Think about a good time had a long time ago,
Think about, forget about your troubles and your woes.
Walkin' in the sunshine, sing a little sunshine song.
Whether the weather be rain or snow,
Pretendin' can make it real,
A snowy pasture, a green and grassy field.
Walkin' in the sunshine, sing a little sunshine,
Walkin' in the sunshine, sing a little sunshine song.

YOU'VE GOT A FRIEND

Words and Music by Carole King

When you're down and troubled and you need some
    love and care,
And nothing is going right,
Close your eyes and think of me and soon I will be there
To brighten up even your darkest night.

Refrain:
You just call out my name and you know wherever I am,
I'll come runnin' to see you again.
Winter spring summer or fall,
All you have to do is call,
And I'll be there. You've got a friend

If the sky above you grows dark and full of clouds
And that ol' northwind begins to blow,
Keep your head together and call my name out loud;
Soon you'll hear me knockin' at your door. *(Refrain)*

How many times did you need to hear this song before you
    could sing it yourself?
Where did the song state ideas of despair? hope?
How did the music help express these ideas?

3

THE POWER AND GLORY

Words and Music by Phil Ochs

When you first hear a recording of a new song, what first attracts your ear?
WORDS?   MELODY?   RHYTHM?   HARMONY?
ACCOMPANYING INSTRUMENTS?
several of these?   all of these?

C'mon and take a walk with me through this green
and growin' land,
Walk through the meadows and the mountains and the sand,
Walk through the valleys and the rivers and the plains,
Walk through the sun and walk through the rain.

Refrain:
Here's a land full of power and glory
Beauty that words cannot recall.
Oh, her power shall rest on the strength of her freedom,
Her glory shall rest on us all.

From Colorado, Kansas and the Carolinas, too.
Virginia and Alaska from the old to the new,
Texas and Ohio and the California shore.
Tell me, who could ask for more. *(Refrain)*

Yet she's only as rich as the poorest of the poor,
Only as free as a padlocked prison door,
Only as strong as our love for this land,
Only as tall as we stand. *(Refrain)*

YOU'RE A GRAND OLD FLAG

Words and Music by George M. Cohan

Listen to this song. Write down what first attracts your attention. Be prepared to discuss your reactions.

You're a grand old flag, you're a high flying flag;
And forever in peace may you wave;
You're the emblem of the land I love,
The home of the free and the brave.
Every heart beats true under red, white, and blue,
Where there's never a boast or brag;
But should auld acquaintance be forgot,
Keep your eye on the grand old flag.

WHAT DO YOU HEAR?

When someone speaks to you, what do you hear?

sounds?   words?   ideas?   feelings?

How many different feelings and ideas can you communicate by using just one of these word patterns?

Hello!

Hi!

Watch Out!

See ya later!

All Right!

Where'ya goin'?

So Long!

Now...PLAY MUSICALLY WITH WORDS

Use Pitch

As you speak these phrases again, copy the up and down motion of your voice on pitched wooden instruments.

Use

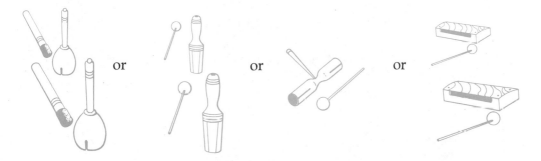

or   or   or

Use Other Musical Elements

Select a leader to speak each of these patterns.
The class must echo the leader.

Accent

STOP! QUIT!
RUN! JUMP!

Rhythm

Hey man, what's the plan?
All right! Outa sight!

Dynamic Changes

Hey! Where'ya goin' with my pencil?
  (class echoes)
Give it back! Give it back!
  (class echoes)
Oh! Here's my pencil on my desk.
  (class echoes)
Sorry 'bout that!
  (class echoes)

- Create other speech patterns to communicate your ideas.
- Select a leader to improvise word patterns and speak them dramatically.
- The class must echo the leader.
- Discuss how the speaker used various musical elements to help express different ideas and feelings.

WHY, OH WHY?

Words and Music by Woody Guthrie

Read this rhyme over and over. Read it as expressively as possible.

Why, oh why, oh why, oh why?
Why, oh why, oh why?
Because, because, because, because,
Goodbye, goodbye, goodbye.

Did you use musical elements in your reading?
Listen to Woody Guthrie's musical setting of these words.
Listen until you can sing the song.

LOWER VOICES:

Why, oh why, oh why, oh why?

HIGHER VOICES:

Why, oh why, oh why? Because, because because, because.

Goodbye, goodbye, goodbye!

Why can't a dish break a hammer?

Why, oh why, oh why? Because a hammer's a hard head,

Goodbye, goodbye, goodbye!

Why can't a bird eat an elephant?

Why, oh why, oh why? Because an elephant's got a pretty hard skin.

Goodbye, goodbye, goodbye!

Why does a horn make music?

Why, oh why, oh why? Because the horn-blower blows it,

Goodbye, goodbye, goodbye!

Why don't you answer my questions?

Why, oh why, oh why? Because I don't know the answers.

Goodbye, goodbye, goodbye!

What Do You Really Hear?

Listen again to the songs you learned at the beginning of this unit. This time pay close attention to the way musical elements help express the words. What are you *really* hearing?

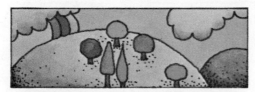

GONNA BUILD A MOUNTAIN

WALKIN' IN THE SUNSHINE

WHY, OH WHY?

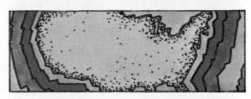

THE POWER AND GLORY

YOU'VE GOT A FRIEND

YOU'RE A GRAND OLD FLAG

Could the lyrics have "stood alone"? Which musical elements helped express the messages?

MELODY — In what ways does the melody support important ideas? How are important words stressed by pitch changes?

RHYTHM — In what ways does the rhythm reinforce important ideas? In what ways does the rhythm stress important words?

STRUCTURE — Are certain musical ideas repeated? Is the number of musical ideas the same as the number of word ideas? What about the lengths of musical ideas?

MUSICIAL CONTROLS — How do tone quality, dynamics, and articulation help express the messages?

Did you notice other musical elements that helped express the messages?

ANN STREET

Words by Maurice Morris   Music by Charles Ives

How does this composer use musical elements to express the ideas of the words?

Broadway
Quaint name,
   Ann Street
width of same,
   ten feet.
Barnums mob,
   Ann Street
far from obsolete
   Narrow, yes,
Ann Street
   But business,
both feet.
   Nassau crosses
Ann Street
   Sun just hits
Ann Street,
   then it quits—
some greet!
   Rather short,
Ann Street...

Express Your Own Ideas
...through Words ...through Music

WHICH?

Poem by Brenda Lee Jenkins   Music by Buryl Red

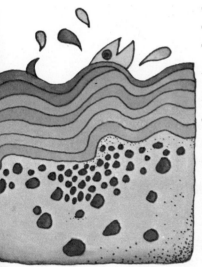

Down from the mountain
In from the sea
Rocks and pebbles are tossed
Mindlessly.

The pebble was gnashed
Til' it finally wore round.
The rock still pierces
And punctures the ground.

Which would I be,
The pebble or rock?
Could I be both
Or would I be mocked?

Down from the mountain
In from the sea
Rocks and pebbles are tossed
Mindlessly.

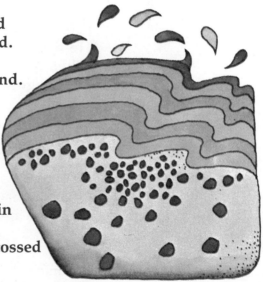

Brenda Lee expressed her thoughts very well just by using words. Listen as someone reads the poem aloud. Which musical elements do you find in the word patterns?

Listen to a composer's musical setting of Brenda Lee's poem. As you listen, write down ways you think the music helped express the words. Be prepared to discuss your ideas.

Everyone has important ideas and feelings. Express one or more of yours in writing. You do not need to use rhyming words unless you want to. Could you use musical sounds or a melody to help express your idea?

Learn Harmonies by Hearing

When listening to music a musician hears many things besides melody and words. As you listen to the next three songs, listen specifically for things that are happening in the accompaniment part.

ME AND MY CAPTAIN

Traditional

Me and my captain don't agree,
But he don't know 'cause he don't ask me.

Refrain:
He don't know, he don't know my mind.
When he sees me laughin',
Just laughin' to keep from cryin.'

Got one mind for the captain to see,
Another for what I know is me.
(Refrain)

One of these days and it won't be long,
He'll call my name but I'll be gone.
(Refrain)

Did the accompaniment use one, two, or three chords?

WORRIED MAN

American Folk Song

It takes a worried man to sing a worried song.
It takes a worried man to sing a worried song.
It takes a worried man to sing a worried song.
I'm worried now, but I won't be worried long.

The guitarist accompanied each verse of this song with the following chord sequence:

G   C   G   D7   G

Can you hear the chord changes played on the guitar?
Slide your finger from one chord symbol to the next each time you hear the chords change.

Learn to sing and play this song by listening. Use a guitar, autoharp, or ukulele.

I WALK THE UNFREQUENTED ROAD

Words by Frederick L. Hosmer   American Folk Hymn

I walk the unfrequented road
With open eye and ear;
I watch afield the farmer load
The bounty of the year.

A beauty springtime never knew
Haunts all the quiet ways,
And sweeter shines the landscape thro'
Its veil of autumn haze.

I face the hills, the streams, the woods
And feel with all akin;
My heart expands; their fortitude
And peace and joy flow in.

Slide your finger from chord to chord as you hear this accompaniment repeated for each verse:

Gm   Dm   Gm   Dm   Gm   Dm   Gm

Learn by hearing to play this accompaniment.

HEARING ONE SOUND AMONG MANY

Hey! Ho! Anybody home?
Meat and drink and money have I none.
Still I will be very merry,
Hey! Ho! Anybody home!

Sit in a circle and close your eyes. Listen to a chord played on an instrument. Send the sounds of this chord around the circle.

The First Time Choose one person to begin. "Pull" one sound from the many you hear. Sing it on "loo."
Sustain your pitch for as long as you wish.
When you are ready to stop singing, tap your neighbor gently. That person must now pull a different sound from the chord. Continue around the circle.

The Second Time Begin as before. This time, when you signal your neighbor, continue to sustain your pitch. Take a breath whenever you need it, but come back in on the same pitch.
Some class members can now sing the familiar song "Hey Ho, Anybody Home," while others continue to sustain the sounds they have pulled from the chord.

The Third Time Begin as before, but this time each person must "embroider" the pitch in some way:
Begin with your chosen pitch; then move your voice higher or lower. Try to improvise a short melody pattern. End by returning to your original pitch.
Again send this idea around the circle.

Sing "Hey Ho" again. This time try having different soloists perform their improvised melodies as interludes between repetitions of the song.

Engage in your "pulling sounds" activity again. Choose, then sustain, the sounds of the chord you hear.

This time the accompanist will change chords.

Can you change to a neighboring tone that sounds right with the new chord? Can you move back and forth between the two chords?

Now listen to "Sometimes I Feel Like a Motherless Child" until you can sing the melody.

SOMETIMES I FEEL LIKE A MOTHERLESS CHILD

American Folk Song

Listen closely to the accompaniment. It uses the two chords you've just practiced. Can you hear when the chord changes occur?

Sometimes I feel like a motherless child,
Sometimes I feel like a motherless child,
Sometimes I feel like a motherless child,
A long way from home, a long way from home.

HALLELUJAH CHORUS

from *Messiah*

By Georg Friedrich Handel

Hallelujah! Hallelujah!
For the Lord God Omnipotent reigneth.
The kingdom of this world is become
The Kingdom of our Lord and of His Christ;
And He shall reign forever and ever.
King of Kings and Lord of Lords.

This selection for chorus is 4 minutes long. It contains only the words given above. Will you be able to learn this song just by listening to it?

As you listen, follow this "musical map." Listen for call numbers.

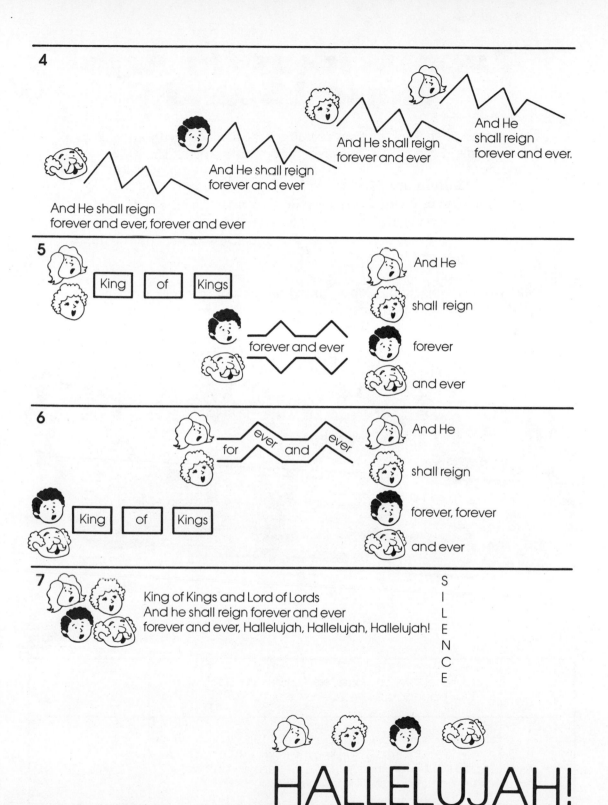

4

And He shall reign
forever and ever, forever and ever

And He shall reign
forever and ever

And He shall reign
forever and ever

And He
shall reign
forever and ever.

5

King | of | Kings

forever and ever

And He

shall reign

forever

and ever

6

for ever and ever

King | of | Kings

And He

shall reign

forever, forever

and ever

7

King of Kings and Lord of Lords
And he shall reign forever and ever
forever and ever, Hallelujah, Hallelujah, Hallelujah!

SILENCE

HALLELUJAH!

Express Ideas through Musical Sound

Sometimes music tells a story or suggests a mood without any help from words. Such music is called "program" music. The story is the "program."

The statements below describe a trip down a river. List the order in which you think the events might occur if you were taking such a trip. Think of ways each event might be suggested in musical sound. Then, compose your own program music.

Plan your composition. Choose instruments and practice until you are satisfied with your performance. Tape record your piece. Then play it for your classmates. Can they identify your "program"?

My Program		Smetana's Program
	a I travel through huge forests, trees on each side. A fox appears, followed by hunters.	
	b As my boat floats through the night, the waters become so calm that I can see the reflections of castles and towers from the shore. The reflections in the water remind me of days of kings, queens and knights.	

18

	c Water from a sparkling spring starts its trip toward the sea.	
	d Watch out! The rapids are ahead! Will I make it through? The waves foam up; the roar of the rapids is deafening!	
	e Other streams join the first, some calm and quiet, others sparkling and chattering.	
	f Night comes on; the water nymphs dance on the river's glittering waters, shining in the moonlight.	
	g As the stream goes down the mountainside it becomes bigger and bigger, until finally it becomes a mighty river.	
	h I've made it through the rapids! The river flows on, broad and majestic, toward the city Prague.	
	i My trip is at an end, but the river continues on its journey toward the sea.	
	j On my boat, I pass a village where a wedding is being celebrated with music, song and dance.	

THE MOLDAU

By Bedřich Smetana

The composer Bedřich Smetana created a musical trip using the same program you used in creating your music.

Listen to Smetana's piece. Reread the statements describing the events. As you listen to the music, numbers will be called. As each number is announced, write down the letter of the statement you think the composer is describing. Is his program in the same order as yours?

Unit II
LEARN BY READING

Imagine you lived at a time when there were no radios, no tape recorders, no television sets, and no phonographs. If you found this song in a book in the library, how would you learn it?

THE WABASH CANNONBALL

    G   C

From the great Atlantic Ocean to the wide Pacific shore,

     D7   G

'Cross the queen of flowing rivers, over mountains by the score,

   G   C

It's long and tall and handsome, it's known by one and all,

    D7   G

It's a modern combination called the Wabash Cannonball.

Were you able to sing the song? Did everyone agree on how it should sound?

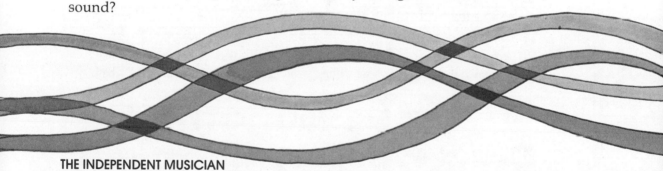

THE INDEPENDENT MUSICIAN

Which of these can you now do independently?			
read melodies from notation	read rhythms from notation	read harmonies from notation	perform melodies, rhythms, and harmonies
In which areas will you commit yourself to becoming more independent?			

WABASH CANNONBALL

American Folk Song

1. From the great At-lan-tic O-cean to the wide Pa-cif-ic shore, 'cross the
2. Come and lis-ten to the jin-gle, to the rum-ble and the roar, as it's

queen of flow-ing riv-ers, o-ver moun-tains by the score, It's
rid-ing through the wood-lands, to the hills and by the shore, The

long and tall and hand-some, it's known by one and all, It's a
mag-ic of the rail-road wins praise from one and all, As we

mod-ern com-bi-na-tion called the Wa-bash Can-non-ball.
trav-el 'cross the na-tion on the Wa-bash Can-non-ball.

Make Your Own Bluegrass Arrangement

You can organize your own bluegrass band, similar to the one heard on the recording. Almost any instruments you have can be used, or try adding some real "homemade" instruments.

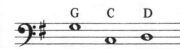 Play these chord roots on your "tuned jugs" on the first beats of appropriate measures.

Pluck this pattern.

Add a "walking bass" on the piano.

Fill in beats two and four with chords on piano or autoharp.

Try these "finger-picking patterns"; play chord tones, one after the other, on ukulele, guitar, or autoharp.

Add a rhythm section.

Someone who plays violin can "saw" these open fifths.

Play these patterns on bells to imitate a "slide guitar."

Here is the introduction played on the recording. Use the instruments you have assembled to develop your own introduction. Later, try improvising your own bluegrass arrangements on your favorite country songs.

Read Melody

There are several ways to read a melody. One way is to relate the tones of the melody to the steps of the scale.

Start on one
of these pitches.

Sing a major scale up and down
with numbers.

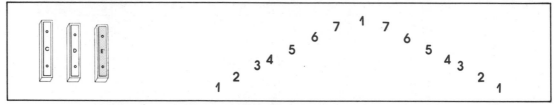

Now, try some patterns.

Play the first pitch on bells or piano. Sing the pattern. Then check yourself by playing the whole pattern on bells.

YOUR COMMITMENT TO LEARNING

Which of these can you now do independently?	
read melodies by following numbers and music notation	read melodies in relation to chord structure and scale organization
In which areas will you commit yourself to becoming more independent?	

WHEN I FIRST CAME TO THIS LAND

American Ballad

Use your understanding of scale steps to learn this song. Begin by chanting the words in rhythm, stressing the *accented* words.

Then practice singing the scale.

D	E	F♯	G	A	B	C♯	D
1	2	3	4	5	6	7	1

Now sing the song using the numbers of the scale steps.

Verse:

```
              5   5   6 6   5   4 5
          3                       3
      1                       1   2   7 1
When I first came to this land, I was not a wealth-y man.
```

```
          5 5 6 6 5
      3             4        5 5
  1                     2            1
So I got myself a farm, I did what I could.
```

```
      3 4 4 3
  1            2 2 2 2
                      1
And I called my farm "mus-cle in my arm."
```

```
          5 5 6   6   5
      3                 3 4      5 5
  1                         2        1
But the land was sweet and good and I did what I could.
```

Refrain: But the land was sweet and good and I did what I could.

ADD VERSES:

So I built myself a shack, I did what I could.
And I called my shack "break my back."

So I got myself a cow . . . and I called my cow, "no milk now."

So I got myself a horse . . . and I called my horse, "horse of course."

So I got myself a wife . . . and I called my wife, "love of my life."

So I got myself a son . . . and I called my son, "my work's done."

Check yourself by listening to the recording. Was your melody correct?

BOIL THAT CABBAGE DOWN

American Folk Song

Now use your ability to sing with scale numbers to learn a song from staff notation.

Listen to the recording. How well did you read from staff notation?

STREETS OF LAREDO

Cowboy Song

As you sing this song with numbers, accompany yourself on the autoharp.
Listen to the way the melody and the accompaniment "go together."

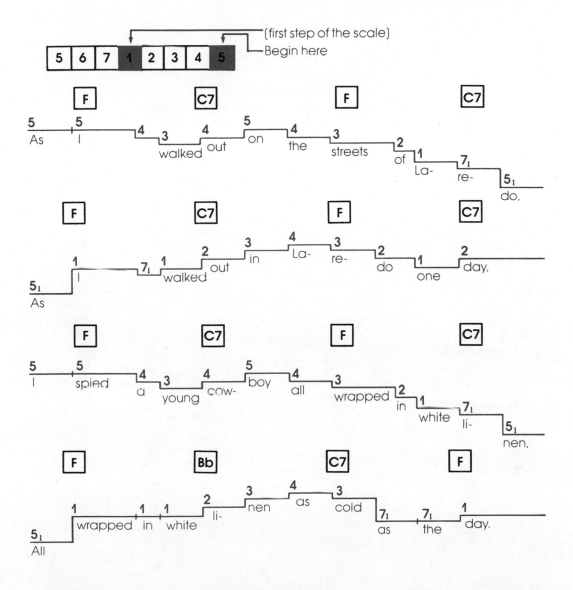

Did the sounds of the changing chords help you to find the tones of the melody?

Melody and Mood

SYMPHONIE FANTASTIQUE
Fourth movement

by Hector Berlioz

Listen to this composition several times.

THE FIRST TIME: Think about the different moods suggested.

THE SECOND TIME: Follow the "musical map." Notice the character of each melody.
Does it move mostly by steps? by skips?
mostly downward? mostly upward?
Is it based on a major scale? a minor scale?
Is the melody usually low in pitch? usually high?
Is the range narrow or wide?

THE THIRD TIME: Think about how the character of the melody helps to shape the mood of each section.

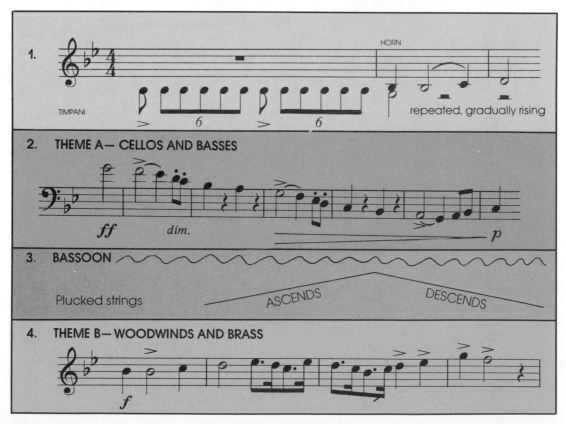

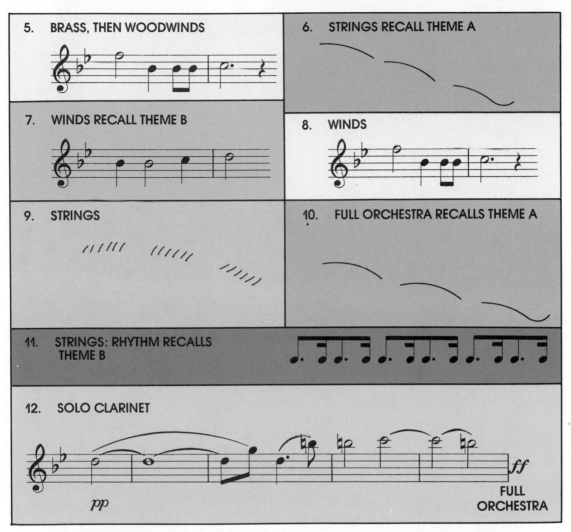

5. BRASS, THEN WOODWINDS

6. STRINGS RECALL THEME A

7. WINDS RECALL THEME B

8. WINDS

9. STRINGS

10. FULL ORCHESTRA RECALLS THEME A

11. STRINGS: RHYTHM RECALLS THEME B

12. SOLO CLARINET

pp

ff

FULL ORCHESTRA

The title of this movement is "March to the Scaffold." Each movement of this symphony tells part of a story. Here is the composer's description of this part.

The artist dreams that he has killed his beloved. He dreams that he is condemned and led to the scaffold, and that he is witnessing his own execution. The procession moves forward to the sounds of a march that is now somber and fierce, now brilliant and solemn, in which the muffled noise of heavy steps gives way to the noisiest clamor. At the end of the march, the first four measures of the beloved's theme appear, like a last thought of love, interrupted by the fatal blow.

Listen again. How do the themes help "tell the story"? What other musical elements contribute to the mood of this music?

29

A Challenge

Can you hear the low, middle, and high tones in a chord? Can you sing those tones as a melodic pattern? See how well you do. Play this game in pairs or take turns in a group.

CHORD SENDER

1. Play one of the chords in box 1, striking all three bells at the same time.

2. Check the sound finder by playing the pattern.

SOUND FINDER

1. Listen, then sing the tones of the chord following the order of the disks in box 1.

2. Correct any errors.

3. Choose a chord from box 2 and continue playing the game!

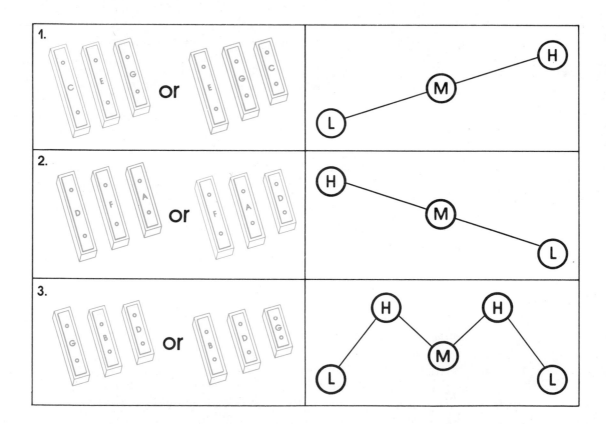

Make up additional patterns to challenge your partner.

COMPOSE YOUR OWN MELODY

Make up your own melody, using any combination of the

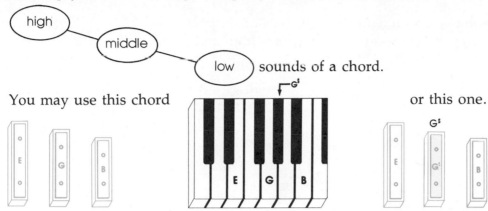

high middle low sounds of a chord.

You may use this chord or this one.

The chord might be played on bells, piano, guitar, or autoharp.

Before you begin composing your melody, chant the lyrics several times to get the feel of the rhythm.

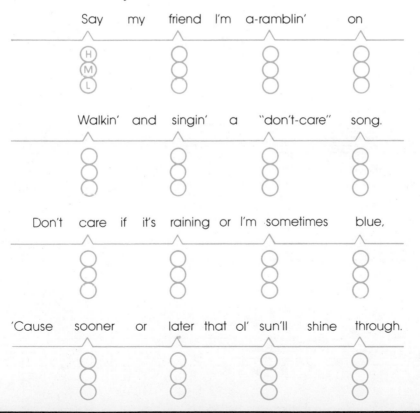

Say   my   friend   I'm   a-ramblin'   on

Walkin'   and   singin'   a   "don't-care"   song.

Don't   care   if   it's   raining   or   I'm   sometimes   blue,

'Cause   sooner   or   later   that   ol'   sun'll   shine   through.

SONG SUNG BLUE

Words and Music by Neil Diamond

Song writers often build melodies on chordal tones.
Listen to this song. Can you find chordal patterns in the melody?

Song sung blue, ev-'ry-bod-y knows one. Song sung
blue, ev-'ry gar-den grows one. Me and you ___
___ are sub-ject to ___ the blues now and then, ___ but,
when you take the blues and make a song ___ you sing them out a-gain, ___
Sing them out a-gain. ___ Song (song) sung (sung)
blue (blue) weep-in' like a wil-low, Song (song) sung (sung)

blue (blue) sleep - in' on my pil - low.   Fun - ny thing ___

___ but you can sing ___ it with a   cry in your voice ___

And be - fore you know it start to feel - in' good ___

___   you sim - ply got no choice.

These are the chords that are used in this song.

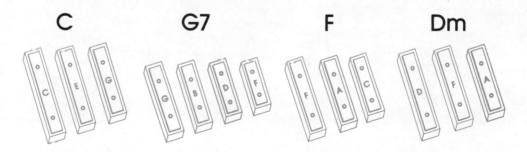

Can you improvise a melodic pattern at the end of each phrase, using the tones of an appropriate chord?

Try improvising a pattern on the bells. Then try creating a vocal improvisation.

THE HERMITAGE
by Joan Miro

The Hermitage by Joan Miro.
The Philadelphia Museum of Art.

Improvise music that reflects the way lines, shapes, and colors are organized in this painting.

Which artistic element will you represent by melody? which by harmony?

Chords and Melody Go Together

When singing songs with scale numbers, you found that melodies sometimes move by steps, sometimes by skips. These skips are often made up of the low, middle, and high tones of chords.

Use the skill you gained when playing "A Challenge" to learn this melody by following the chordal patterns.

Play these chords.   Sing this melody.

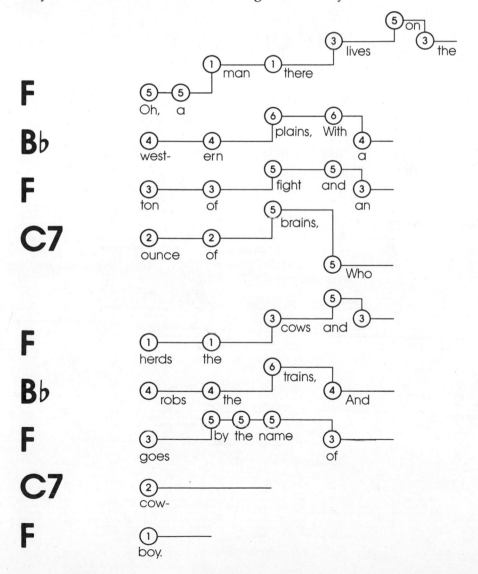

F

B♭

F

C7

F

B♭

F

C7

F

THE COWBOY

American Folk Song

Here is "The Cowboy" written in traditional staff notation.

How does the notation help you to know that this melody is based entirely on chordal tones?

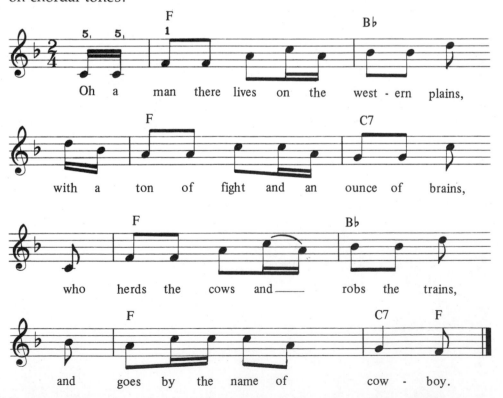

Oh a man there lives on the west-ern plains,

with a ton of fight and an ounce of brains,

who herds the cows and —— robs the trains,

and goes by the name of cow - boy.

A HUNDRED YEARS AGO

American Windlass Song

This melody is based on these two chords:

Put a clear sheet of plastic over your song page.

Mark the melodic contour by circling a note each time the melody moves up or down.

Examine the notes you've marked. Can you find patterns based on the tones of these chords?

Sing the basic melodic contour on "loo." Then sing the song with words as you accompany with bells, autoharp, or guitar.

1. A hun - dred years is a ver - y long time,
2. A hun - dred years have passed and gone,
3. A hun - dred years will come once more,

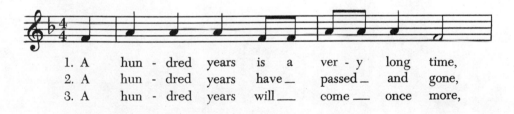

Oh, yes, oh! A hun - dred years is a
Oh, yes, oh! A hun - dred years have
Oh, yes, oh! A hun - dred years will

ver - y long time, A hun - dred years a - go.
passed and gone, A hun - dred years a - go.
come once more, A hun - dred years a - go.

WHY, OH WHY?

Words and Music by Woody Guthrie

This melody is based
on these two chords.

Here are the same chords
"stretched out."

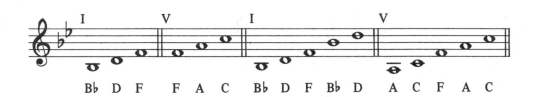

Bb D F   F A C   Bb D F Bb D   A C F A C

Practice singing the "stretched-out" patterns. Can you locate these higher
and lower tones in the song?

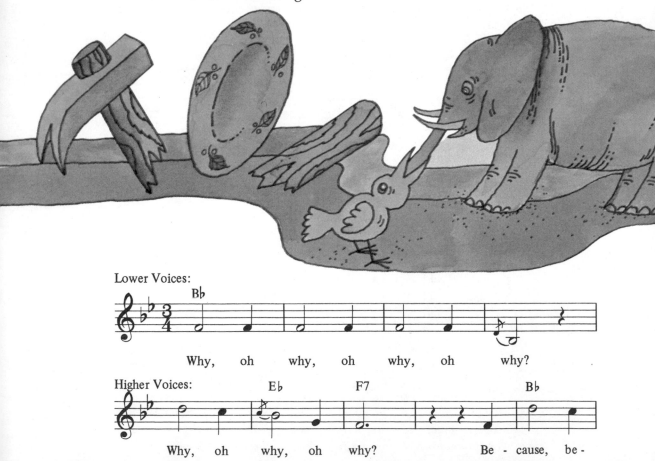

Lower Voices:

Bb

Why,   oh   why,   oh   why,   oh   why?

Higher Voices:

Eb   F7   Bb

Why,   oh   why,   oh   why?   Be - cause, be -

cause, be - cause, be - cause,____ Good - bye, good -

bye,____ good - bye.____

1. Why can't a   dish break a
2. Why can't a   bird eat an
3. Why does a   horn____ make
4. Why don't you an - swer my

Higher Voices:

ham - mer?____
ele - phant?____
mu - sic?____
ques - tions?____

Why, oh why, oh why?

Lower Voices:

Be - cause a ham-mer's a   hard   head,____
Be - cause an el - e - phant's got a pret-ty hard skin,
Be - cause the horn-blow - er   blows   it.____
Be - cause I don't know the   an - swers.____

Good-

bye, good - bye,____ good - bye.____

AS THE SUN GOES DOWN

Words and Music by Josef Marais

Many songs combine passages that move by scale steps with passages that are based on chordal tones. In this song, most of the patterns are drawn from these three chords.

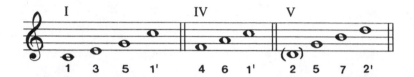

Put a clear sheet of plastic over the musical notation of the song. Locate patterns based on these three chords. Circle each chordal pattern with a different color.

Locate patterns that seem to be based on scale steps. Circle those with a fourth color.

Did you find notes in the scale patterns that pass between two tones of a chord? These are called **passing tones.**

Practice singing the song as you play the chords. Sing on "loo" or with numbers first. Then sing the words.

sun goes down, Down, down be - low the moun - tain.
sun comes up, Up, up a - bove the moun - tain.

Refrain

I'll ride, I'll ride, I'll ride, I'll ride, I'll ride all night, When the

moon is bright, When the moon is bright; I'll

ride, I'll ride, I'll ride, I'll ride, I'll ride all night,

D.C. al Fine

I'll get there in the morn - ing.

Merced River, Yosemite Valley by Albert Bierstadt (1830-1902, United States).
Oil on canvas, 36″ × 50″. The Metropolitan Museum of Art, New York. Gift of the sons of William Paton, 1909.

IF...THEN

IF this is a

	C	C#/Db	D	D#/Eb	E	F	F#/Gb	G	G#/Ab	A	A#/Bb	B	C
CHROMATIC SCALE	C	C#/Db	D	D#/Eb	E	F	F#/Gb	G	G#/Ab	A	A#/Bb	B	C
MAJOR SCALE	C		D		E	F		G		A		B	C
MINOR SCALE	C		D	E♭		F		G	A♭		B♭		C
PENTATONIC SCALE	C		D		E			G		A			C
WHOLE-TONE SCALE	C		D		E		F♯		G♯		A♯		C

THEN can you. . .

. . . describe two ways that all scales are the *same*?

. . . describe two ways in which each is *different*?

. . . make a definition of a scale?

Can you make up your own scale? Use six different pitches. Play your scale. Have the class decide whether it meets the definition of a scale.

Play this tune, using the pitches of your new scale.

1   2   3   1   1   2   3   1   3   4   5   3   4   5

5 6 5 4 3   1   5 6 5 4 3   1   1   5   1   1   5   1

FARANDOLE

from *L'Arlésienne Suite No. 2*

by Georges Bizet

"Farandole" is based on two themes. One theme is based on a major scale. The other is based on a minor scale. Can you identify each?

Listen until each theme has been introduced. Decide which you think is major and which is minor.

THEME I

THEME 2

Listen again. Make a chart that shows the sequence of the themes.

At one point in the composition, the minor theme is played in the major mode. Can you tell when this occurs?

Pick a Scale

To read a new song, you need to know the scale on which it is based. As you learn the songs on the following pages, go through the steps listed below. Determine the scale on which each song is based.

1. Find the "tonal center" of the melody, often the final tone.

2. Write out a chromatic scale beginning with that tone.

3. Find all the different pitches in the song. Write their names below the chromatic scale.

4. Compare the pattern of whole and half steps you've arranged with the patterns in the box on page 42. Which scale does it match?

EVERYBODY LOVES SATURDAY NIGHT

African Folk Song

Ev- ery- bod - y   loves   Sat - ur - day   night. _____
Mo- fe mo - ni   s'mo   ho ____ gbe - ke. _____

Ev- ery- bod - y   loves   Sat - ur - day   night. _____
Mo- fe mo - ni   s'mo   ho ____ gbe - ke. _____

Ev-ery-bod- y,   ev-ery-bod- y,   ev-ery-bod- y,   ev-ery-bod- y,
Mo-fe mo -ni,   mo-fe mo - ni,   mo-fe mo - ni,   mo -fe mo - ni,

Ev- ery - bod - y   loves   Sat - ur - day   night. _____
Mo- fe   mo - ni   s'mo   ho ____ gbe - ke. _____

44

SHALOM ALËHEM

Jewish Folk Song

Repeat steps 1-4 to discover the scale of this song.

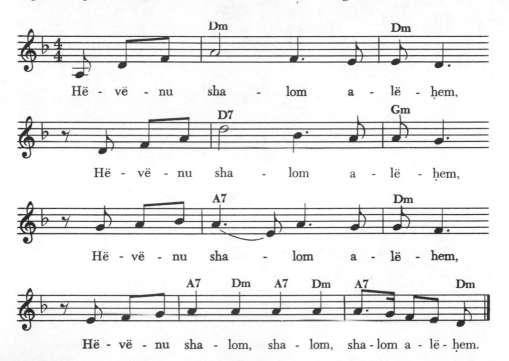

Hë - vë - nu sha - lom a - lë - ḥem,

Hë - vë - nu sha - lom a - lë - ḥem,

Hë - vë - nu sha - lom a - lë - ḥem,

Hë - vë - nu sha - lom, sha - lom, sha - lom a - lë - ḥem.

ARIRANG

Words Adapted

Korean Folk Song

Before you begin to learn this song, follow the steps on page 44 to determine the scale on which it is based.

1. A - ri - rang, _ A - ri - rang, _ A - ri - rang, _ A - ri - rang, _
2. A - ri - rang, _ A - ri - rang, _ A - ri - rang, _ A - ri - rang, _

A - ri - rang, _ A - ri - rang, _ A - ri - rang fair.
A - ri - rang, _ A - ri - rang, _ A - ri - rang fair.

Through the pass _ I watch you _ go _ there. _____
Here I wait for you, wait, wait _ and _ stare. _____

A - ri - rang, _ A - ri - rang, _ A - ri - rang fair.
A - ri - rang, _ A - ri - rang, _ A - ri - rang fair.

THE CAGE

Words and Music by Charles Ives

A leopard went around his cage
from one side to the other side, he stopped
only when the keeper came around with meat.
A boy who had been there three hours began to wonder —
Is life anything like that?

What kind of a melody would you compose for this poem? Would you use any special musical elements to help express the feelings and ideas of the story?

Compose a melody for this poem based on the following scale. Use the tones of the scale to add harmony to your melody.

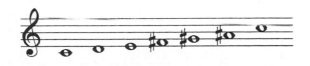

Listen to a setting of this poem by the composer Charles Ives. He used the same scale that you used as the basis for his song.

Did Ives organize any other musical elements in the same way you did?

JOHNNY HAS GONE FOR A SOLDIER

American Folk Song

Can you determine the scale on which this song is based?

Can you find patterns based on any of these chords in this song?

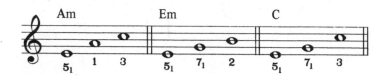

Practice the patterns. Then sing the melody.

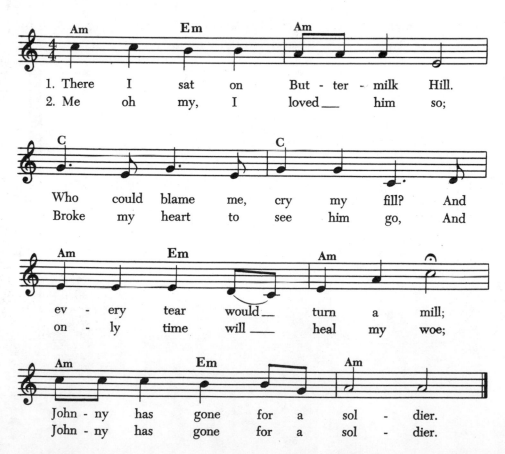

1. There I sat on But - ter - milk Hill.
2. Me oh my, I loved___ him so;

Who could blame me, cry my fill? And
Broke my heart to see him go, And

ev - ery tear would___ turn a mill;
on - ly time will ___ heal my woe;

John - ny has gone for a sol - dier.
John - ny has gone for a sol - dier.

In Unit I you practiced singing chords by first listening to the chords played on instruments. Here is a new challenge. Can you sing this chord sequence by following the numbers? Can you decide when to change to a new chord?

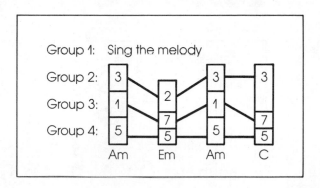

Group 1:   Sing the melody

Group 2:   3   3   3

Group 3:   1   2   1

Group 4:   5   7   7
               5   5   5

           Am   Em   Am   C

The Departure by K. A. Lamb.
Addison Gallery, Andover, Massachusetts. Photo by John King.

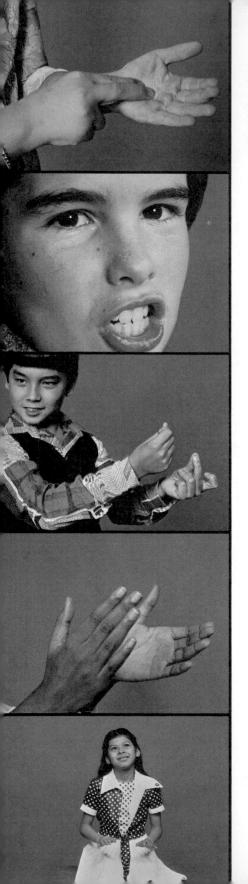

Read Rhythm

Group I	①	②	③	④	⑤	⑥	⑦	⑧
Group II	①	②	③	4	5	⑥	⑦	⑧
Group III	1	2	③	4	5	⑥	⑦	8
Group IV	①	2	3	④	⑤	⑥	⑦	8
Group V	①	②	3	④	⑤	6	⑦	8

Each number represents one short sound. Perform the patterns, making sounds only on the circled numbers.

Follow the pictures for sound ideas.

Add each group one at a time and repeat the patterns over and over.

Perform these patterns as an accompaniment to "Saturday Night."

YOUR COMMITMENT TO LEARNING

Which of these can you now do independently?		
read rhythms from notation	do rhythmic addition	hear and identify rhythms in compositions
In which areas will you commit yourself to becoming more independent?		

THE SET DRUMMER

Here is another group of rhythms for you to perform. A set drummer might use patterns like these for the rhythm section of a jazz combo.

1. Begin with the "cymbal stick." Lightly tap your right hand against your right leg.

①②③④⑤⑥⑦⑧①②③④⑤⑥⑦⑧

2. Add the bass drum part with your right foot.

① 2 3 4 ⑤ 6 7 8 ① 2 3 4 ⑤ 6 7 8

3. Add the high-hat cymbal rhythm playing "off beats" with left foot.

1 2 ③ 4 5 6 ⑦ 8 1 2 ③ 4 5 6 ⑦ 8

4. Finally, add the snare drum part with your left hand against left leg.

1 2 ③ 4 5 6 ⑦ ⑧ 1 2 ③ 4 5 6 ⑦ ⑧

Here is a score of the patterns you are playing.

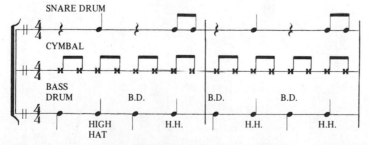

Perform your set drum part as you listen to "Peter Gunn." Do you hear any of your patterns performed by the drummer?

PETER GUNN

by Henry Mancini

This music begins with a series of short sounds:

① ② ③ ④ ⑤ ⑥ ⑦ ⑧ ① ② ③ ④ ⑤ ⑥ ⑦ ⑧

accompanied by the snare drum in this rhythm.

1 2 ③ 4 5 6 ⑦ 8 1 2 ③ 4 5 6 ⑦ 8

Other instruments from the rhythm section pick up the repeated rhythm. They add a repeated melody, or *ostinato*.

Listen for the bass entrance that occurs at the same time:

(1 2) 3 4 5 6 7 8 (1 2) 3 4 5 6 7 8

(1 2) (3 4) (5 6) (7 8) (1 2) (3 4) (5 6) (7 8)

Listen for the entrance of the brass section. Can you show this rhythm?

Add a Rhythm

Can you add

$$1 + 1 = ?$$

$$2 + 2 = ?$$

$$4 + 4 = ?$$

Then you can do musical addition!

Learn the rhythm of a new song by
adding the short sounds together.
Begin with a series of short sounds.
Brush a pencil eraser back and forth on the desk—

or lightly tap with your fingertips.

Now perform the rhythm of the song in relation to
this series of short sounds.

Remember to follow the musical "plus" signs!

Add two sounds together   or four sounds.

Down the road just a | mile or two |

Match the accompaniment.   Add three sounds.

lives a lit - tle girl named | Pearl - y Blue, A -

Complete the song.

bout so high and her | hair is brown, the

pret - ti - est thing, boys, | in this town.

DOWN THE ROAD

American Folk Song

Did you figure out the rhythm of "Down the Road" by adding the short sounds together? Here is the same song in traditional notation.

Down the road just a mile or two

lives a lit - tle girl named Pearl - y Blue, A -

bout so high and her hair is brown, the

pret - ti - est thing, boys, in this town.

OLD ABRAM BROWN

Words Anonymous   Music by Benjamin Britten

This song moves mostly with short sounds. When will you need to add two short sounds together?

This sign 𝄾 means "be silent" for one short sound.

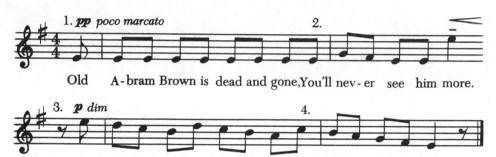

Old A-bram Brown is dead and gone, You'll nev-er see him more.

He used to wear a long brown coat That but-toned down be-fore.

MORE ADDITION

Choose a partner. Raise your left hand and hold it steady.

Partner A: Tap your partner's left palm with your right palm in the rhythm of the song.

A - bram   Brown   is   dead   and   gone,   You'll

Partner B: Tap your partner's left palm with your right palm, but make each sound TWICE AS LONG.

A - bram   Brown   is

Can you sing the melody in your rhythm while you continue to send and receive rhythms by clapping?

55

COME, FOLLOW ME

Round by John Hilton

Study the rhythm of "Come Follow Me" as it is shown in the musical notation on the next page. Then demonstrate your ability to do musical addition.

Put a clear sheet of plastic over the box below. Connect the short notes with musical "plus" signs to equal the rhythm of the melody. The first measure is already done for you.

Learn the song. Follow the same steps you completed when learning "Down the Road."

1.
Come, fol - low, fol - low, fol - low, Fol - low, fol - low,

2.
fol - low me! Whith - er shall I fol - low, fol - low, fol - low,

Whith - er shall I fol - low, fol - low thee? To the green - wood,

3.
to the green - wood, To the green - wood, green - wood tree.

Hallecord

Learn this Creole dance phrase by phrase. Then dance to the music!

STEP! HOP! **SIDE—BACK—SIDE**

PUSH STEP

Create your own instrumental
accompaniment by following
the dancers' movements.

Select a master drummer.

Find the shortest sound and play it
continuously on the maracas.

You'll need a group to play thudding
and clicking sounds,

and a group to play metallic sounds.

SHUCKIN' OF THE CORN

American Folk Song

Listen to the recording.
Half the class should tap
the shortest sounds.

The rest should tap the beat.

Notice that there are two short sounds for every beat and that the beats move in twos.

Review the way to discover the beat grouping, or **meter,** of a song. Do you recall the clue in the musical score that tells you which note will move with the beat?

Some musical "plus" signs have already been included in this score. When they appear in the notation, they are called **ties.**

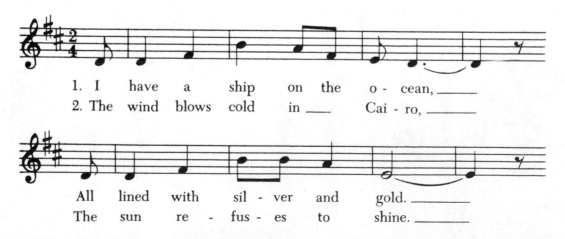

1. I   have   a   ship   on   the   o - cean, _____
2. The   wind   blows   cold   in ___   Cai - ro, _____

All   lined   with   sil - ver   and   gold. _____
The   sun   re - fus - es   to   shine. _____

Which section of the song moves mostly with the shortest unit of sound? Which moves mostly with the beat? What is the difference in "feel" between these two sections?

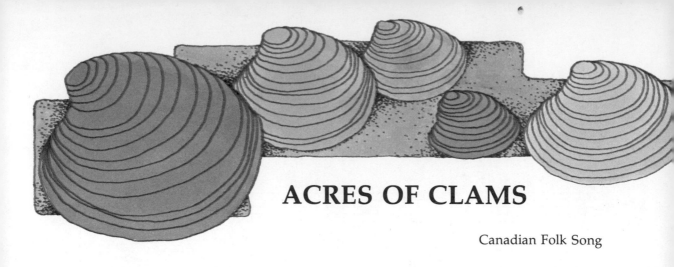

ACRES OF CLAMS

Canadian Folk Song

In some songs, the shortest unit of sound that you feel is also the beat.
How will beats be grouped in this song?

Can you find the musical "plus" signs in this song?
This plus sign is called a **tie**.

This sign is called a **slur**.
What difference do you notice?

1. I've wan-dered all   o - ver this coun-try, _____   Pros -
2. For each who got   rich - es   by   min - ing, _____   I
3. I   rolled up   my   grub in   my   blan - ket, _____   I

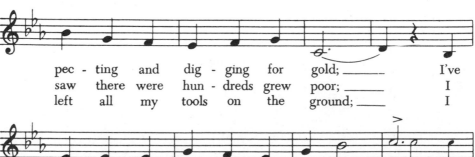

pec - ting   and   dig - ging   for   gold; _____   I've
saw   there   were   hun - dreds   grew   poor; _____   I
left   all   my   tools   on   the   ground; _____   I

tun - neled, hy - drau - licked, and   cra - dled,   And
made   up   my   mind   to   try   farm - ing,   The
start - ed   one   morn - ing   to   shank it   For   the

I have been fre - quent - ly sold, _____ And
on - ly pur - suit that is sure, _____ The
coun - try they call Pu - get Sound, _____ For the

I have been fre - quent - ly sold, _____ And
on - ly pur - suit that is sure, _____ The
coun - try they call Pu - get Sound, _____ For the

I have been fre - quent - ly sold. _____ I've
on - ly pur - suit that is sure. _____ I
coun - try they call Pu - get Sound. _____ I

tun - neled, hy - drau - licked, and cra - dled, And
made up my mind to try farm - ing, The
start - ed one morn - ing to shank it For the

I have been fre - quent - ly sold. _____
on - ly pur - suit that is sure. _____
coun - try they call Pu - get Sound. _____

4. No longer the slave of ambition,
   I laugh at the world and its shams;
   And think of my happy condition
   Surrounded by acres of clams.
   Surrounded by acres of clams,
   Surrounded by acres of clams.
   And think of my happy condition
   Surrounded by acres of clams.

63

BRAZILIAN DANCE

from Three Dances for Orchestra

by Camargo Guarnieri

Much of the excitement of this lively samba comes from its driving rhythms based on short sounds. Listen to the whole dance. As you listen, try lightly tapping the shortest sounds.

Can you continue to sense the shortest sounds even when they are not heard in the music?

Richard Steedman/The Image Bank

This entire composition is based on two thematic ideas.

Theme 1   1 2 3 4 5 ⑥⑦⑧①②③④⑤⑥⑦⑧①②③④⑤⑥⑦⑧

Accompaniment   ①②③④⑤⑥⑦⑧①②③④⑤⑥⑦⑧①②③④⑤⑥⑦⑧

Listen to the dance again. As you listen to the opening section, try tapping either the rhythm of the theme or the rhythm of the accompaniment.

Can you hear the introduction of the second theme? It is played first by trombones. This time the driving pattern of short sounds is in the accompaniment.

Theme 2   1 2 3 4 5 6 ⑦⑧①②③④⑤⑥⑦⑧①②③④⑤⑥⑦⑧

Accompaniment   ①②③④⑤⑥⑦⑧①②③④⑤⑥⑦⑧①②③④⑤⑥⑦⑧

Near the middle of the composition, the strings play the most complete statement of Theme 2. Is the accompaniment the same as before?

Prepare a "musical map" of this composition, showing when each theme is heard. Will your map ever show ideas from both themes at the same time?

BLOW THE WIND SOUTHERLY

Northumberland Folk Song

As you listen to this song, you can tap the short sounds: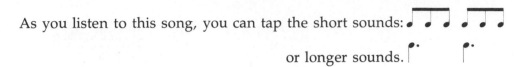

or longer sounds.

What is the relationship of the short sound to the longer sound?

Blow the wind south- er - ly, south- er - ly, south- er - ly,

1. Blow the wind south o'er the bon - ny blue sea;
2. Blow, bon - ny breeze o'er the bon - ny blue sea;

Blow the wind south - er - ly, south - er - ly, south- er - ly,

Blow, bon - ny breeze,— my lov - er to me. They
Blow, bon - ny breeze,— and bring him to me.

told me last night there were ships in the off - ing, And
Is it not sweet — to hear the breeze sing - ing, As

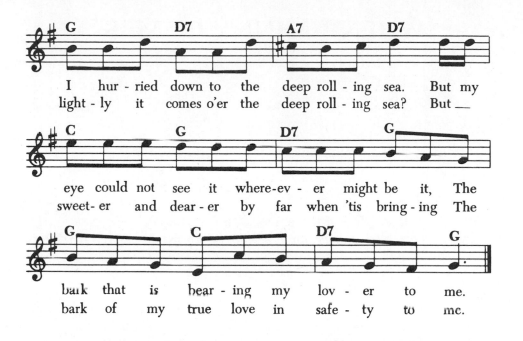

I hur - ried down to the deep roll - ing sea. But my
light - ly it comes o'er the deep roll - ing sea? But —

eye could not see it where-ev - er might be it, The
sweet- er and dear - er by far when 'tis bring - ing The

bark that is bear - ing my lov - er to me.
bark of my true love in safe - ty to me.

Girl with Red Stockings; The Wreck by Winslow Homer.
Bequest of John T. Spaulding. Courtesy Museum of Fine Arts, Boston.

WHEN JOHNNY COMES MARCHING HOME

Words and Music by Louis Lambert

As you listen to this song, you can tap the short sounds:

or the beats.

What is the relationship of the short sound to the beat?
The meter signature of this song would probably be clearer if it were written this way: **2.**   Why do you suppose it isn't?

| Gm | Gm | Bb |

1. When John - ny comes march-ing home a - gain, Hur - rah! ___ Hur-
2. The old ___ church bell will peal with joy, Hur - rah! ___ Hur-

| Bb | Gm | Gm |

rah! ___ We'll give him a heart - y wel - come then, Hur -
rah! ___ To wel - come home our dar - ling boy, Hur -

| Bb | Bb | Bb |

rah! ___ Hur - rah! ___ The __ men will cheer, __ the
rah! ___ Hur - rah! ___ The __ vil - lage lads ___ and

| F | Gm | D7 |

boys will shout, The la - dies, they __ will all turn out, } And we'll
lass - ies gay, With ros - es they __ will strew the way, }

| Gm | D7 | Gm | D7 | Gm | Gm |

all feel gay When John - ny comes march - ing home. ___

68

BATTLE HYMN OF THE REPUBLIC

Music Attributed to William Steffe

Words by Julia Ward Howe

In this song, this note represents the shortest sound:

The dotted pattern may seem difficult, but you can figure it out by adding short sounds!

Mine eyes have seen the glo - ry of the com - ing of the Lord; He is tram-pling out the vin - tage where the grapes of wrath are stored; He hath loosed the fate-ful light-ning of His ter - ri - ble swift sword; His truth is march - ing on.

Refrain: Glo - ry, glo - ry, hal - le - lu - jah! Glo - ry, glo - ry, hal - le - lu - jah! Glo - ry, glo - ry, hal - le - lu - jah! His truth is march - ing on.

WATER COME A ME EYE

Words Adapted   Jamaican Folk Song

Listen to the recording. Get the "feel" of the short sounds, played on the maracas. Then try softly chanting the rhythm of the words with the short sounds.

If you're not sure of your musical addition, stop and figure it out. How many short sounds will you add together to equal this note?

This sign ⸘ means "be silent." How many short sounds will you leave out?

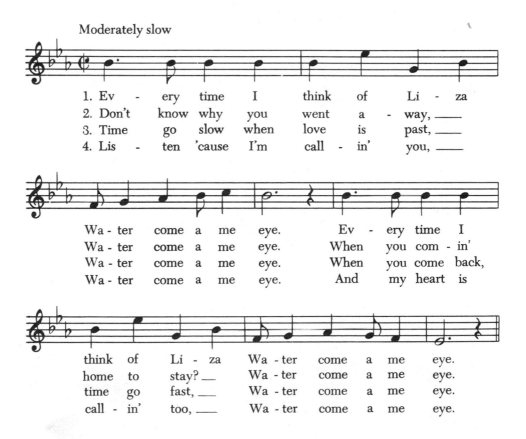

Moderately slow

1. Ev - ery time I think of Li - za
2. Don't know why you went a - way, ___
3. Time go slow when love is past, ___
4. Lis - ten 'cause I'm call - in' you, ___

Wa - ter come a me eye. Ev - ery time I
Wa - ter come a me eye. When you com - in'
Wa - ter come a me eye. When you come back,
Wa - ter come a me eye. And my heart is

think of Li - za Wa - ter come a me eye.
home to stay? ___ Wa - ter come a me eye.
time go fast, ___ Wa - ter come a me eye.
call - in' too, ___ Wa - ter come a me eye.

Folksinger by Hartwell Yeargans.
Lithograph from Prints by American Negro Artists, T. V. Roelof-Lanner, Editor, 1967. Courtesy, Cultural Exchange Center Publishers, Los Angeles, Cal.

Refrain

Come back, Li - za, come back girl, Wa - ter come a me eye.

Come back, Li - za, come back girl, Wa - ter come a me eye.

HAND-CLAPPING CHOIR

Choirs are usually made up of soprano, alto, tenor, and bass voices. Here is a composition for soprano, alto, tenor, and bass hand-claps! You can produce the different pitch levels by clapping in these special ways.

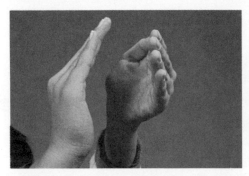

BASS CLAP

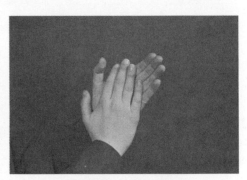

TENOR CLAP

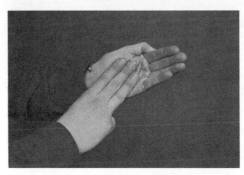

ALTO CLAP

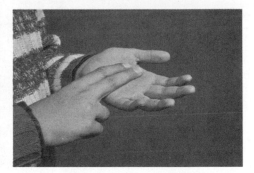

SOPRANO CLAP

Form a hand-clapping choir and perform the composition on the next page.

Sopranos set the tempo by tapping the pattern of short sounds.

Basses enter next. They establish the meter by accenting the first beat of each measure.

Read the other patterns in relation to the short sounds of the soprano line.

Now add the recorded sounds of the set drums. The set drums will add additional textures as well as more intricate rhythm patterns to your ensemble. Listen to the pattern several times. Then begin.

Work in small groups. Create an original score for hand-clapping choir.

BLACKBIRD

Words and Music by
John Lennon and Paul McCartney

When you first scan this song, the rhythm may look very difficult. But, if you remember how to add, you'll find it's not that hard at all!

Listen to the accompaniment. Find the shortest sound. Determine its relationship to the steady beat.

Did you sense that the short sounds move in 4–1 relation to the beat?

Try using your pencil "brush" technique to keep the short sounds going:

Softly chant the rhythm of the melody as you listen to the accompaniment.

1. 3. Black - bird sing - ing in the dead of night, —
2. Black - bird sing - ing in the dead of night, —

—— Take these brok - en wings —— and learn to fly; ——
—— Take these sunk - en eyes —— and learn to see; ——

—— All your life ————————
—— All your life ————————

you were on - ly wait - ing for this mo - ment to a -
you were on - ly wait - ing for this mo - ment to be

rise.   (2.) free.   (3.) rise.

Black - bird, —— fly, —— Black - bird, — fly ——

———————— in - to the light of a dark, black night. ——

Read Harmony

Harmony results whenever two strands of sound occur at the same time. Learn to sing "This Old Hammer." Then make your own arrangement by combining two strands of sound in different ways.
Follow the suggestions on the next page.

THIS OLD HAMMER

American Work Song

This old ham-mer _____ killed John Hen-ry, _____

This old ham-mer _____ killed John Hen-ry, _____

This old ham-mer _____ killed John Hen-ry, _____ But it

won't kill me, _____ won't kill me. _____

YOUR COMMITMENT TO LEARNING

Which of these can you now do independently?			
sing and play harmonies by ear	sing in thirds and sixths	make your own harmonic arrangements	sing polyphonically
In which areas will you commit yourself to becoming more independent?			

Sing a song in **canon.**

This old ham‑mer_____ killed John Hen‑ry

This old ham‑mer_____

Some people with low voices might add a **drone.**

This old ham‑mer *(or)* This old ham‑mer *(or)* This old ham‑mer

Or try an **ostinato,** repeating a pattern like this one over and over.

killed John Hen‑ry John.

Or sing **polyphonically,** by adding another melody that "fits."

Me and my cap‑tain don't a‑gree, But

he don't know 'cause he don't ask me.

Make up other vocal parts or an instrumental accompaniment. If you use an autoharp or guitar, play a G minor chord. On mallet instruments, use these pitches: G B♭ C D E♭.

You've been singing rounds for a long time. Singing in round is one way to produce harmony.

THE SWAN

Traditional Round

Sing this song as a two-part round.

Sweet - ly the swan sings Do- de- ah- do,   do - de -ah- do,   do - de-ah-do.

When the voices are combined,
this harmony results.
The voices are sounding
in **thirds.**

Many rounds produce thirds. Review the following.

"Are You Sleeping?"
"Three Blind Mice"
"Lovely Evening"

Can you tell when the thirds occur?

Sing "The Swan" again, this time as a three-part round. Now the voices are sounding in **triads,** or chords with three pitches. How many thirds are in each triad?

IV   III   II   I

The names of the chords are written in Roman numerals. Why do you suppose they are named IV, III, II, and I?

Thirds and "Upside-Down" Thirds

Now that you have the "sound of thirds" in your ears, try harmonizing this old folk tune in thirds. Start by reviewing the melody.

HUSH LITTLE BABY

Traditional

Hush lit - tle ba - by, don't say a word,
If that mock - ing bird don't sing,

ma - ma's gon - na buy you a mock - ing bird.
ma - ma's gon - na buy you a dia - mond ring.

Now, divide into low voices and high voices.
Everyone begins in **unison** on C.
Low voices continue to sing the melody.
High voices "hop up" to high C on the word "Little" and continue to sing the melody from that pitch.

Try something else.
Begin in unison again.

This time, high voices sing the original melody.
Low voices stay on middle C.
Continue to sing the melody, moving up and down from that pitch.

You've sung "upside down thirds!"
What else might this **interval** be called?

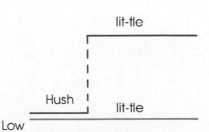

Thirds and Sixths

Experiment with harmonizing other familiar songs by thirds and sixths.

BOIL THAT CABBAGE DOWN (page 26)

During the refrain, the low voices
sing the melody. The high voices sing a
third higher.

Boil that cab - bage

'Pos - sum in a

During the verse, trade parts.
High voices sing the melody.
Low voices sing a third lower.

The second time you sing the refrain,
high voices sing the melody.
Low voices sing a sixth lower.

Boil that cab - bage

WHEN I FIRST CAME TO THIS LAND (page 25)

When I first came

Begin on D. Then sing in thirds.
Return to a **unison** on D at the
end of each phrase.

There's one place where you'll need
to sing a sixth. Can you find it?

BATTLE HYMN OF THE REPUBLIC (page 69)

To harmonize this song you will need both thirds and sixths. Begin with
the low voice singing a third *below* the main melody. Listen carefully!
Your ears will tell you when to switch to singing in sixths! When will
you return to thirds?

Mine eyes have seen the

Parallel Motion

FRENCH CATHEDRALS

Traditional French Round

You've discovered the pleasing sounds that result when you sing in **parallel motion** in thirds or sixths. Try some other intervals. Learn to sing "French Cathedrals" in unison. When you know the melody very well, sing it as a round.

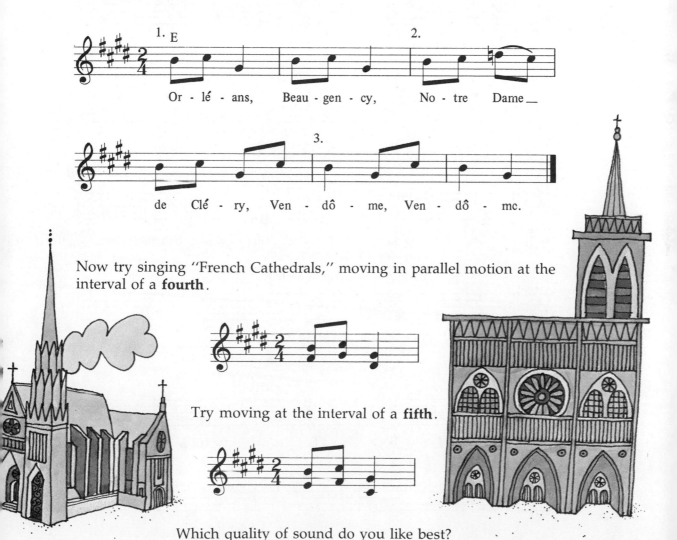

Or - lé - ans, Beau - gen - cy, No - tre Dame de Clé - ry, Ven - dô - me, Ven - dô - mc.

Now try singing "French Cathedrals," moving in parallel motion at the interval of a **fourth**.

Try moving at the interval of a **fifth**.

Which quality of sound do you like best?

DU, DU LIEGST MIR IM HERZEN

Arranged by Mary Val Marsh

German Folk Song

This song moves mostly in thirds. Can you learn to sing it by following the notation? When you've learned the melody and the harmonizing part, a few voices might add the independent melody, or **descant**, during the refrain.

la _____ la la la. _____

Weisst nicht, wie gut ich dir bin. _____

ICELANDIC PRAYER

Icelandic Folk Song

Movement in parallel fifths was one of the earliest kinds of harmony. It was known as **organum.**

This Icelandic prayer is typical of church music of the ninth century.

1. O great God of the earth,
2. O great mak - er of life,

Hear now my prayer ris - ing up - ward,
Give now my spir - it Thy beau - ty,

(Melody in lower part)

Wak - en my soul to Thy good!
Fill all my days with Thy work!

Wak - en my soul to Thy good!
Fill all my days with Thy work!

ROLL ON, COLUMBIA

Words and Music by Woody Guthrie

The harmony part for the refrain of this song is written on a separate staff.

Notice that the voices move mostly in **parallel motion.**

When will you be singing in **contrary motion?**

4. At Bonneville now there are ships in the locks;
   The waters have risen and cleared all the rocks.
   Shiploads of plenty will steam past the docks;
   Roll on, Columbia roll on!
   Refrain

5. And on up the river is Grand Coulee Dam,
   The mightiest thing ever built by a man,
   To run the great fact'ries and water the land;
   Roll on, Columbia, roll on!
   Refrain

GLOCKENJODLER

Arranged by Egon Kraus   Austrian Folk Song

Although this song is written in four parts, you'll find it easy to learn. The two upper voices move consistently in thirds, while the two lower voices provide a drone. What **intervals** do the drone voices produce?

From the Ground Up!

Listen to three different compositions played by

a mariachi band   a string orchestra   an African "High Life" ensemble.

All have something in common. Can you hear what it is?

CLUE: Listen closely to the parts played by the accompanying voices.

LA CACHIPORRA

by Moncada-Matos

DEATH OF FALSTAFF
from *Henry V*

by Sir William Walton

AWUBEN

by Faka Acquaye

Did you discover that each piece is based on a repeated pattern, or **ground?** This kind of pattern is also called an **ostinato.**

Listen to each composition several times. What differences do you notice in the ways the different ostinatos are used?

TURN YE TO ME

Words by John Wilson   Scottish Folk Song

Make an arrangement of "Turn Ye to Me" by combining two of the harmonic styles you've already learned.

Phrases 1 through 4: While most voices sing the melody, a few low voices may add a drone to suggest Scottish bagpipes. Notice that this part is written in **bass clef.**

Brumm   brumm   brumm   brumm

Phrases 5 through 7: Change to this harmonic ostinato.

Blow   wind,   blow   wind

Phrase 8: Return to the first drone.

1. The stars are shin - ing cheer - i - ly, cheer - i - ly,
2. The waves are danc - ing mer - ri - ly, mer - ri - ly,

Walkin' the Bass Line

HE'S GOT THE WHOLE WORLD IN HIS HANDS

Spiritual

1. He's got the whole world in his hands, He's got the
2. He's got the wind and rain in his hands, He's got the
3. He's got both you and me in his hands, He's got both

whole world in his hands, He's got the whole world
wind and rain in his hands, He's got the wind and rain
you and me in his hands, He's got both you and me

in his hands, He's got the whole world in his hands.
in his hands, He's got the whole world in his hands.
in his hands, He's got the whole world in his hands.

Add a harmonizing part by listening to the bass accompaniment. Find the roots of the chords. Sing them on neutral syllables, or with words from the song.

Try adding bass-line accompaniments to these songs. You'll need to listen carefully to know when to change from one pitch to another.

WORRIED MAN BLUES

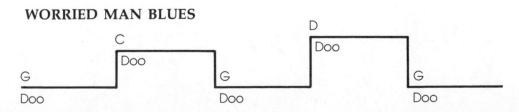

90

BATTLE HYMN OF THE REPUBLIC

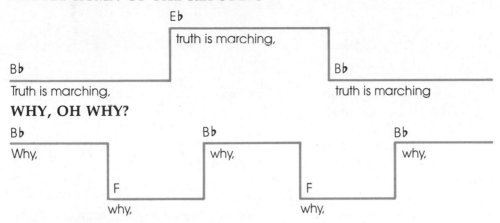

WHY, OH WHY?

Add interest to your bass-line accompaniment by "walking the bass" up and down between the chord roots. . .

WHY, OH WHY?

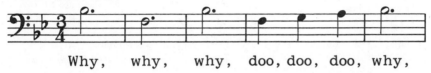

Why,   why,   why,   doo, doo, doo,   why,

HE'S GOT THE WHOLE WORLD IN HIS HANDS

. . . or by outlining the chords you're singing.

BATTLE HYMN OF THE REPUBLIC

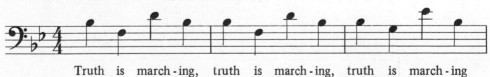

Truth is march-ing, truth is march-ing, truth is march-ing

Often you will need to alter your "walking bass" pattern at the end of the song. Listen carefully. Can you alter it to fit "by ear"?

TZENA, TZENA

Words by Mitchell Parish   Music by I. Miron and J. Grossman

You can create **polyphony** with this unison song by singing the three sections at the same time.

When you know the song well, sing it as a three-part round. Divide into three groups. As one group reaches the second section, the next group begins the first section.

The three sections sound well together because all are based on the same sequence of chords.

Section 3.

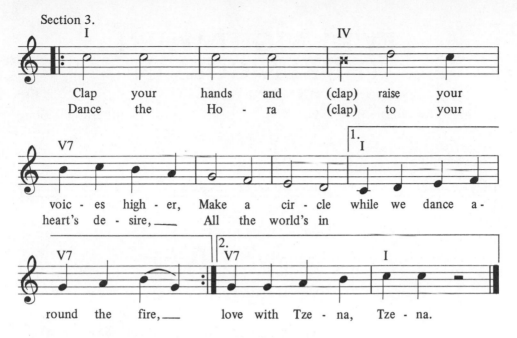

Clap your hands and (clap) raise your
Dance the Ho - ra (clap) to your

voic - es high - er, Make a cir - cle while we dance a-
heart's de - sire, ___ All the world's in

1. I

2. V7   I

round the fire, ___ love with Tze - na, Tze - na.

This song is accompanied with three chords: I, IV, and V7.
Can you figure out the pitches that belong to each chord?

Begin by figuring out the name of each chord. It will be the name of the
first, or root, pitch of the chord.

Find the names of the other notes by "piling up" thirds.

I   IV   V7

Now that you know which pitches to use for each chord, improvise an
instrumental accompaniment on guitar, autoharp, or bells.

93

EV'RY NIGHT WHEN
THE SUN GOES IN

Arranged by William S. Haynie

Southern Folk Song

Ev - 'ry night when the sun goes
Love, don't weep

night _____ when the sun goes in, _____
weep _____ nor _ mourn for me, _____

in, Hang my head
me, Goin' a - way

_ I hang down my head _____ and mourn-ful
_ I'm go - ing a - way _____ to Mar - ble -

1.
and mourn-ful cry.
to Mar - ble -

2.
town.

cry. _____ 2. True love, don't
town. _____

Try another accompaniment to this song. Divide into four groups. Three groups sing harmonic accompaniment; the fourth sings melody.

Doo doo doo doo. Doo doo doo doo. Doo doo doo doo. (Ev - 'ry)

Unit III
CREATE...
DESCRIBE

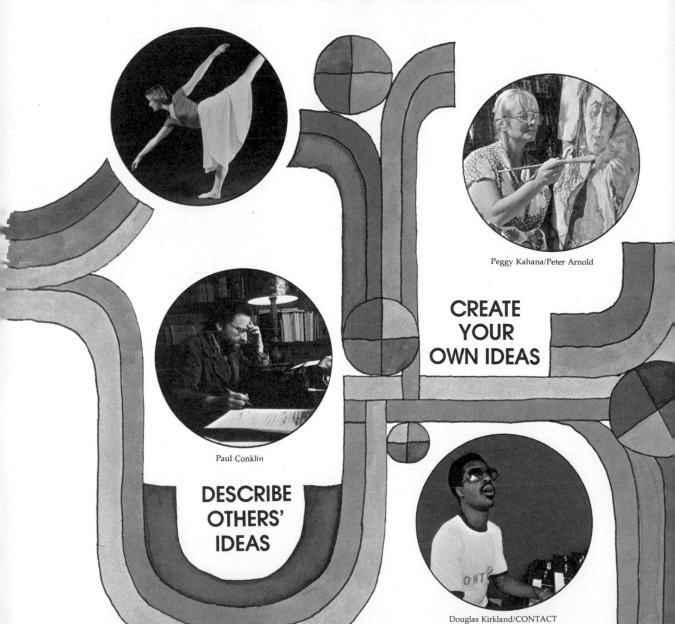

Peggy Kahana/Peter Arnold

CREATE
YOUR
OWN IDEAS

Paul Conklin

DESCRIBE
OTHERS'
IDEAS

Douglas Kirkland/CONTACT

The composer expresses ideas by **creating** a piece of music.

The listener responds to musical ideas by **describing** them with:

WORDS

VISUAL IMAGES

MOVEMENTS

Listen to a composition by Toru Takemitsu. Choose the method of description you like best. Join other students who chose the same method. Develop a description of the music.

Share your descriptions with other groups. Did everyone hear the same things in the music? Did everyone respond in the same way?

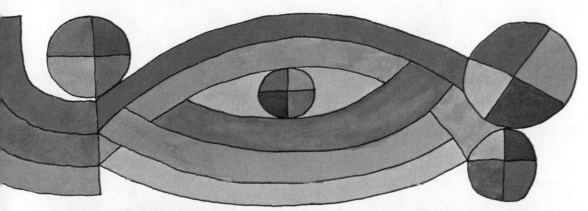

THE INDEPENDENT MUSICIAN

Which of these can you now do independently?			
respond to music with words, visual images, or gestures	describe how musical ideas are combined in a composition	identify the ways a musical idea can be varied, extended	organize your own musical ideas in a composition
In which areas will you commit yourself to becoming more independent?			

The Artist Develops Ideas through Color, Shape and Line

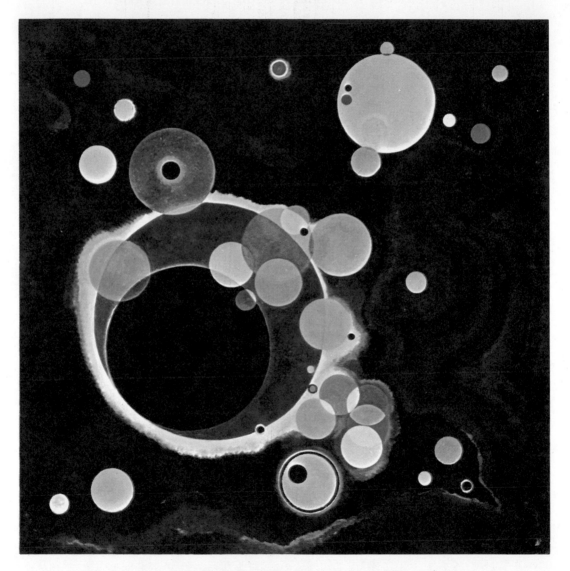

Several Circles, No. 323, 1926, by Vasily Kandinsky (1866-1944, Russia, Germany).
Oil on canvas. Courtesy, The Solomon R. Guggenheim Museum, New York.

Notice how the artist begins with a single idea and extends it into a complete work of art.

The Composer Develops Ideas through SOUND

JOLLY POLKA

from *Mala Suite*

by Witold Lutoslawski

Follow the call numbers as you listen to "Jolly Polka." Notice how the composer begins with a single musical idea and extends it into a complete composition.

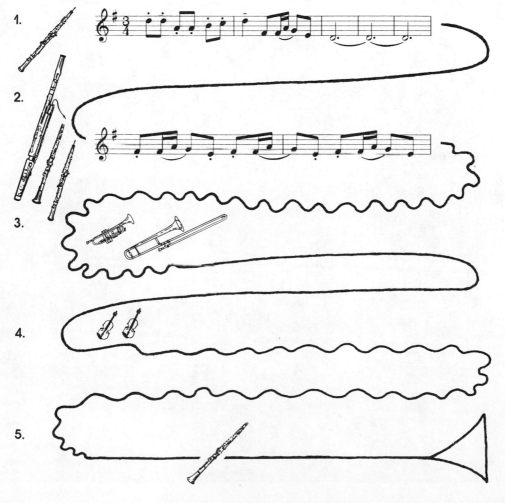

Th Danc r D v lops I as through MOVEMENT

Notice that the dancer begins with a single movement idea and extends it into a series of movements.

The Poet Develops Ideas through WORDS

Read the poem. Notice how the poet begins with a single idea and extends it into a complete poem.

BEAUTY

by E-Yeh-Shure

Beauty is seen
In the sunlight,
The trees, the birds,
Corn growing and people working
Or dancing for their harvest.

Beauty is heard
In the night,
Wind sighing, rain falling,
Or a singer chanting
Anything in earnest.

Beauty is in yourself.
Good deeds, happy thoughts
That repeat themselves
In your dreams,
In your work,
And even in your rest.

EXTEND YOUR OWN IDEAS

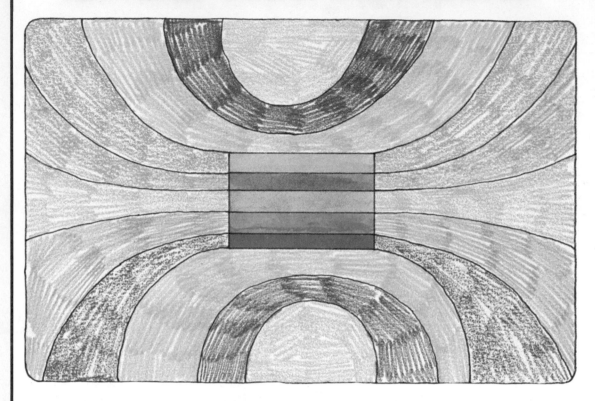

...THROUGH COLORS, SHAPES, AND LINES

Can you find the idea that begins this painting? How is it extended?

Develop your own visual idea.

Find a picture or advertisement that contains an interesting shape or geometric design.

Cut out that small section. Use it as your basic idea.

Paste the shape on a piece of paper in a position that allows you to work "out" from it.

Extend the idea into a complete painting.

...THROUGH MUSICAL SOUND

Begin with this musical idea.

Extend it into a complete composition.

...THROUGH WORDS

Begin with the idea expressed by one of these words.

JOY   FEAR   RED   NIGHT

Create a poem based on your chosen idea.

...THROUGH MOVEMENT

Begin with a single gesture.

Build a dance around this idea. Ask a friend to accompany your dance by improvising patterns on a drum or xylophone.

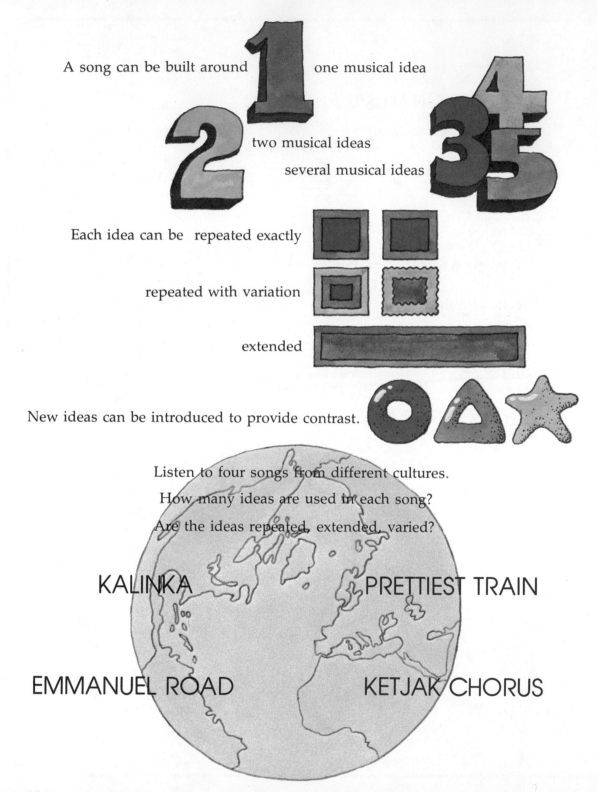

A song can be built around **1** one musical idea

2 two musical ideas

several musical ideas **3 4 5**

Each idea can be repeated exactly

repeated with variation

extended

New ideas can be introduced to provide contrast.

Listen to four songs from different cultures.

How many ideas are used in each song?

Are the ideas repeated, extended, varied?

KALINKA

PRETTIEST TRAIN

EMMANUEL ROAD

KETJAK CHORUS

TAKE TIME IN LIFE

African Dance Song

Learn the musical idea
on which this song is based:

Identify the ways this idea has been repeated, varied, and extended to create the complete song.

Use this information to help you learn to sing the song. Apply the reading skills you have developed.

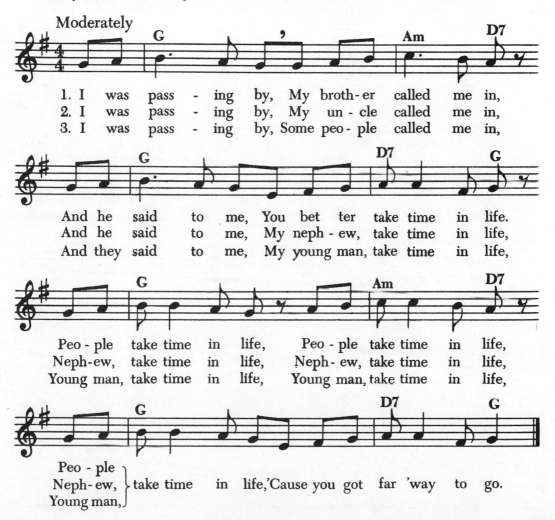

1. I was pass - ing by, My broth-er called me in,
2. I was pass - ing by, My un-cle called me in,
3. I was pass - ing by, Some peo-ple called me in,

And he said to me, You bet ter take time in life.
And he said to me, My neph-ew, take time in life,
And they said to me, My young man, take time in life,

Peo-ple take time in life, Peo-ple take time in life,
Neph-ew, take time in life, Neph-ew, take time in life,
Young man, take time in life, Young man, take time in life,

Peo-ple
Neph-ew, } take time in life, 'Cause you got far 'way to go.
Young man,

SYMPHONY NO. 5

First Movement

by Ludwig van Beethoven

Listen to the way one of the most famous musical ideas of our time is developed into a complete composition.

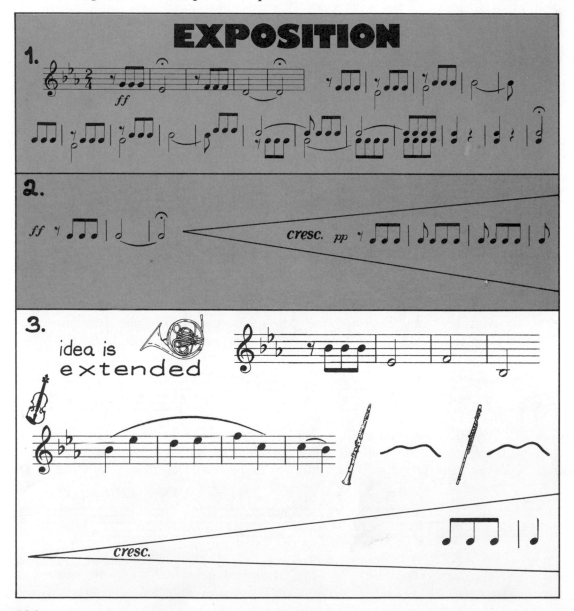

DEVELOPMENT

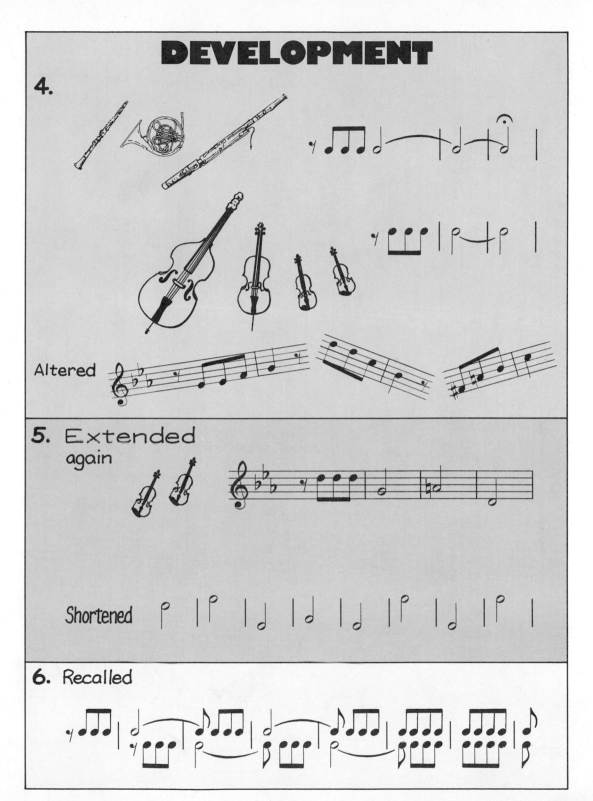

4.

Altered

5. Extended
again

Shortened

6. Recalled

RECAPITULATION

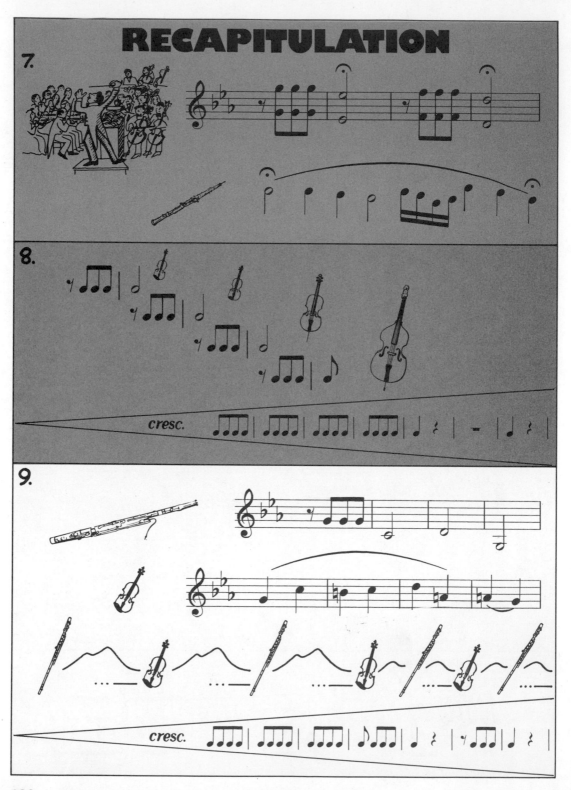

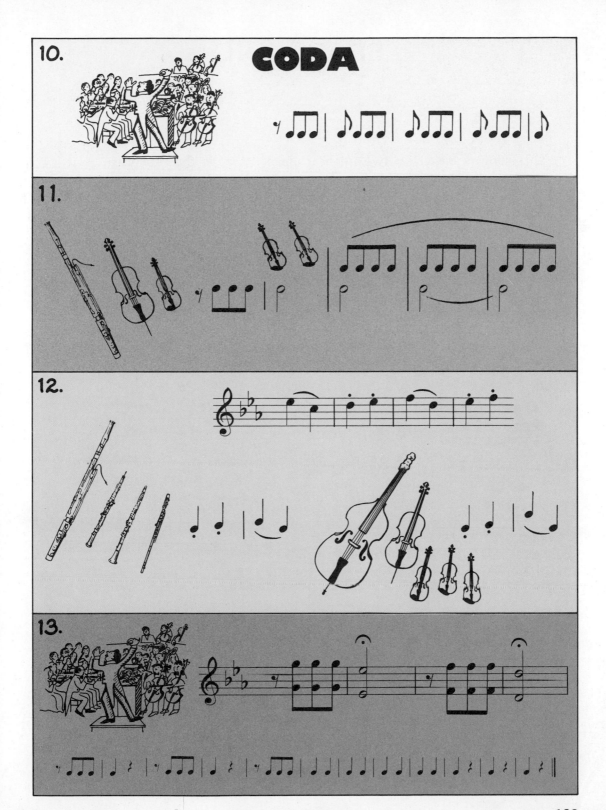

I SHALL SING

Words and Music by
Van Morrison

This song is based on two musical ideas. What is the first idea? Is it repeated, altered, extended?

Locate the second musical idea. Is it treated the same way as the first?

1 and 3. I __ shall sing, __ sing my __ song, __ be it right, __
2. With __ my heart, __ with my __ soul, __ for the young, __

__ be it wrong, __ In __ the night, __ in the __ day __
__ for the old. __ When __ I'm high, __ when I'm low, __

__ an - y - how, __ an - y - way, __ I __ shall sing:
__ when I'm first, __ when I'm slow, __ I __ shall sing:

La la la la la la la la, la la la la la la la. __

__ La la la la la la la la,

la la la la la la la _____ la la la _____ la.

Here is an accompaniment for the song. It consists of two musical ideas. How will you know when to play each? How many times will you repeat each pattern?

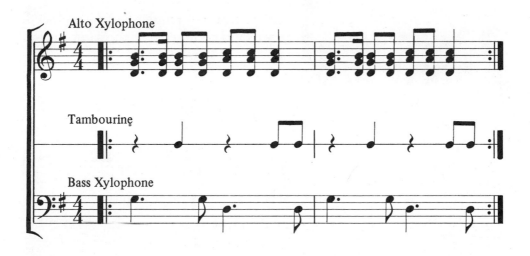

BLUES AIN'T NOTHIN'

Words and Music by Happy Traum

© John Lewis Stage 1978/The Image Bank

How many "word ideas" are expressed in this song?

Is the number of musical ideas the same?

Are the word and musical ideas repeated, varied, and contrasted in the same order?

Well the blues ain't noth - in', no the blues ain't noth - in' but a

good man feel - in' bad, _____ No the

blues ain't noth - in' but a good man feel - in' bad.

it must have been _ those wea - ry blues I had. _

GRIZZLY BEAR

Southern Work Song

Compare the African work song on the next page with this call-response song from the United States.

Verse

1. I'm gon - na tell ___ you a sto - ry 'bout griz - zl - y bear, ___
2. He had ___ great ___ long ___ teeth ___ like a griz - zl - y bear, ___
3. Tell me who ___ was ___ the griz - zl - y bear, ___

___ Jack ___ o' Dia - monds was - n't noth - ing but a griz - zl - y bear. ___
___ He made a track ___ in the bot - tom like a griz - zl - y bear. ___
___ Tell me who ___ was ___ the griz - zl - y bear. ___

Refrain

Oh, ___ the griz - zl - y, ___ griz - zl - y, ___ griz - zl - y bear, ___

___ Oh, ___ the griz - zl - y, ___ griz - zl - y, ___ griz - zl - y bear. ___

Take turns being the leader. Improvise your own "grizzly bear" story, using this melody. Be sure to keep the phrase lengths the same so that the chorus knows when to respond.

MANAMOLELA

English Lyrics by Pete Seeger   South African Work Song

Locate the musical ideas of this "call-response" song. Practice each idea.

Will you use this note ♪ or this ♪ as the underlying pulse? Try tapping each, then decide which seems more helpful.

Leader

Ma - na - mo - le - la, Ma - na - mo -

Chorus

le - - - la, Won't you let us take it slow?___

Won't you let us take it slow?___ Won't you let us

___ Won't you let us take it slow?___ You know the

take it slow? You know the day is long,

day is long, You know the day is long.

You know the day is long, You know the

When you know the two patterns, divide into leader and chorus groups and sing the whole song.

STARRY NIGHT

The title of this painting suggests one idea, a starry night. Does the artist express it by using one, or more, visual ideas?

The Starry Night (1889) by Vincent van Gogh.
Oil on canvas, 29″ × 36¼″. Collection, The Museum of Modern Art, New York. Acquired through the Lillie P. Bliss Bequest.

SWIFT THINGS ARE BEAUTIFUL

by Elizabeth Coatsworth

The title of this poem suggests one idea. After reading the poem, do you agree that only one idea is introduced?

Does the poet repeat one idea? vary it? extend it? Or is she contrasting two ideas?

Swift things are beautiful:
Swallows and deer,
And lightning that falls
Bright-veined and clear,
Rivers and meteors,
Wind in the wheat,
The strong-withered horse,
The runner's sure feet.

And slow things are beautiful;
The closing of day,
The pause of the wave
That curves downward to spray,
The ember that crumbles,
The opening flower,
And the ox that moves on
In the quiet of power.

MOVEMENT
Repetition — Contrast — Unity
"TIME" — A STUDY IN MOVEMENT

by Barbara Haselbach

Repeat this chant many times, becoming gradually faster and faster. One person accompanies on xylophone or piano.

Time   flies.   Time   is   pass - ing   by.

As you sing, form a line. Follow the leader around the floor in a wandering pattern, in the tempo of the chant.

As the tempo increases, detach yourselves from the line, one by one, and sit on the floor. Change from the chant to a hum, using any pitch you like.

When all are seated, stop humming and begin this chant.

For those who live at peace, time is of no im - por - tance.

A soloist may make up a "wandering" melody, using the words of this chant, but in a different rhythm and tempo. Bring the composition to a close by repeating the chant more and more softly. In what ways did this "Study in Movement" use repetition? contrast? Was unity achieved? How?

BOUND FOR THE PROMISED LAND

American Folk Hymn

Use letters of the alphabet to describe the way musical ideas in this song are repeated, varied, or contrasted. The first musical idea is one phrase long; call it **a**. If you find a variation of that idea, call it **a'** (**a** *prime*). What will you call contrasting ideas?

1. On Jor - dan's storm - y banks I stand And
2. There gen - er - ous fruits — that nev - er fall On

cast a wish - ful eye; To____ Ca - naan's fair and
trees im - mor - tal grow; There____ rocks and hills and

hap - py land Where____ my pos - ses - sions lie.
brooks and vales With____ milk and hon - ey flow.

Refrain
I am bound for the prom - ised land, _____ I'm

bound for the prom - ised land; Oh, ____ who will ____ come and

go with me, I am bound for the prom - ised land.

American Novelty Dances

Before you learn these dances, listen to the dance tunes. How long is each musical idea? Can you describe the form?

Move into correct formation. Listen for dance instructions. Learn each dance.

NANA KRU

Liberian Folk Song

Find the three main musical ideas of this song.

Label them a, b, and c.

If you find variations on an idea, add a prime mark: a', b', or c'.

give them two goats, two cows, and six-teen sheep, Jump in - to my

ca-noe, __ Na-na, I paid my dow-ry for you.

AMERICAN SALUTE

by Morton Gould

The musical idea on which a work is based may be a **phrase,** as in "Jolly Polka"; it may be a short motive, as in Symphony No. 5; or it may be a complete small form, as in "American Salute."

The theme of this composition is "When Johnny Comes Marching Home." Review the song, page 68. Describe its form with letters.

Listen to "American Salute." Discover how the small form is extended to create a large form.

The First Time: Listen for the introduction. How many times do you hear the theme? Notice the interludes between statements of the theme.

The Second Time: Which instruments state the theme each time? In what other ways is the theme altered?

The Third Time: Pay particular attention to the accompaniment. Is it the same each time? How is it changed?

Describe what you hear. Develop a "musical map" similar to the one you followed for Symphony No. 5.

The border around this page includes pictures of instruments featured in the music. You may want to copy them for your map.

TUM BALALYKA

Words by Ruth Robbins   Jewish Folk Song

The first musical idea in this song is one phrase long. Can you describe the form of the complete song?

Use lower case letters to identify phrases. The first four phrases form the first section of the song. If you describe this section with a capital **A**, what will you call the second section?

CONSIDER YOURSELF

from *Oliver!*

Words and Music by Lionel Bart

Can you identify the small forms that are combined to create the large form of this show tune?

Moderate march tempo

Con - sid - er your - self ___ at home, ___ Con -

sid - er your - self ___ one of the fam - i - ly. ___ I've

tak - en to you ___ so strong, ___ It's

clear we're go - ing to get a - long! Con -

sid - er your - self ___ well in, ___ Con -

sid - er your - self ___ part of the fur - ni - ture. ___ There

is - n't a lot ___ to spare; ___ Who

cares? What - ev-er we've got we share! {If it should / No-bod-y

chance to be, we should see some hard-er days,___ Emp-ty
tries to be lah - di - dah and up - pit-y,___ There's a

lard - er days,___ why grouse?___ Al - ways a
cup o' tea___ for all.___ On - ly it's

chance we'll meet some-bod-y to foot the bill,___ Then the
wise, to be han-dy with a roll-ing pin___ When the

drinks are on the house!___ }
land - lord comes to call!___ } Con -

sid - er your-self ___ our mate, ___ We

don't want to have ___ no fuss, ___ For

af - ter some con-sid-er-a-tion, we can state: Con -

sid - er your-self ___ one of us.

SUNNY DAY

Words and Music by Donovan Leitch

There are three sections in this song. Can you locate them by studying the score? Label each one with a capital letter.

Describe the form of each section, using a different lower case letter for each idea. Do you notice anything unusual about the forms of these sections?

Sun-ny Day while a - way the af - ter- noon ___

Cut - ting net - tles that are hid - ing pet - als pink

From the riv - er drink. ___ Blue - bells

wood ___ dells where dwells a squir - rel who ___ slinks a -

long branched pat- terns height-ens call of coal - tit small

Spring, 1947, by Ben Shahn (1898-1969, Lithuania, United States).
Oil. Albright-Knox Art Gallery, Buffalo, New York. Room of Contemporary Art.

hov - er o - ver riv - er.

Div - ing, writh - ing, gnatt - ring chiff chaff chat - ter - ing —

Wood - peck - er stag - ger - ing ham - mer - ing —

ex - ag - ger - at - ing his find.

129

EINE KLEINE NACHTMUSIK

Fourth Movement — Rondo

by Wolfgang Amadeus Mozart

In this unit you have examined the ways a composer organizes ideas by:

- repeating, varying, or extending one idea
- introducing contrasting ideas
- combining smaller forms to create a large form

How is this composition for string orchestra organized? Analyze the form of the music. Begin by following the musical score as you listen to the first section.

The music begins with the statement of four ideas.
Each idea is marked in the score with a different color.
Listen to this section several times. When you are familiar with the four ideas, listen to the rest of the work.

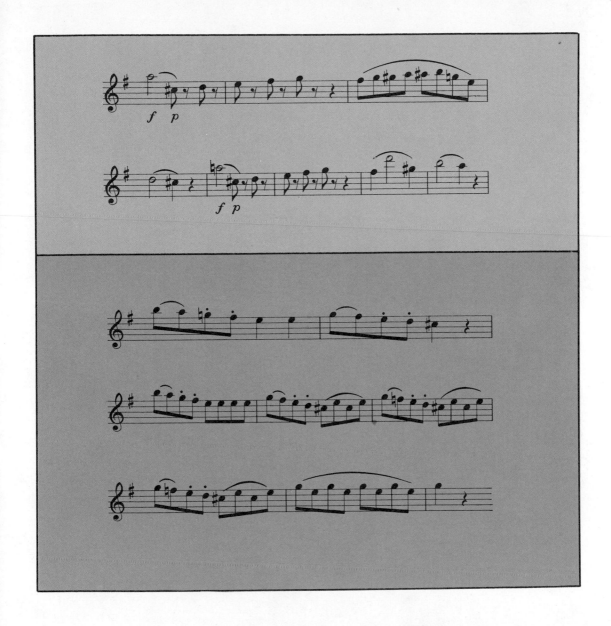

Listen to the rest of the composition. Using the same colors, draw a "line score" to show the order in which the ideas are heard.

This composition is just one movement of a larger work. Listen to the other movements. Discover the form of each.

131

Unit IV
A MUSICIAN PERFORMS

HOW WILL YOU PERFORM?

Make your own kind of music,
Sing your own special song,
Make your own kind of music,
Even if nobody else sings along.

These words describe the special satisfaction of having the musical skills to "make your own kind of music" all by yourself.

When you have these skills, you also have the skills to join with friends and make music together—in duets, small combos, or larger ensembles.

Learn "Make Your Own Kind of Music" in the arrangement that appears on the next three pages. Then experiment with different ways of performing it.

- as a vocal or instrumental solo: melody only
- as a duo: one person on melody, one playing an accompaniment
- in a small combo: a melody "lead," a few accompaniment parts, and a rhythm section
- in a choral setting

THE INDEPENDENT MUSICIAN

Which of these can you now do independently?			
perform on recorder	perform on ukulele	perform in an instrumental ensemble	perform in a choral ensemble
arrange your own vocal or instrumental music		compose your own vocal or instrumental music	
In which areas will you commit yourself to becoming more independent?			

MAKE YOUR OWN KIND OF MUSIC

Words and Music by
Barry Mann and Cynthia Weil

No - bod - y can tell ___ ya; ___
You're gon - na be know - ing ___

There's on - ly one song ___ worth sing - in',
The lone - li - est kind ___ of lone - ly,

They may try and sell ___ ya, ___ 'Cause it
It may be rough go - in', ___ Just to

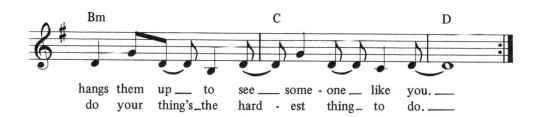

hangs them up ___ to see ___ some - one ___ like you. ___
do your thing's ___ the hard - est thing ___ to do. ___

134

Last time through
repeat chorus and fade

—kind of mu-sic e-ven if no-bod-y else sings a - long.—

—kind of mu-sic e-ven if no-bod-y else sings a - long. —

—kind of mu-sic e-ven if no-bod-y else sings a - long.—

So if you can - not take — my hand, —

And if you must — be go - in', I will un-der-stand. _____

SELF-DIRECTED LEARNING

Recorder

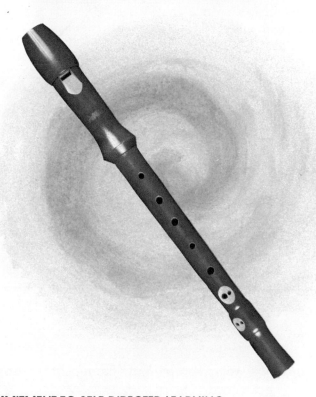

YOUR COMMITMENT TO SELF-DIRECTED LEARNING

Which of these can you now do independently?	
play the recorder in tune	play with rhythmic and melodic accuracy
read musical notation	improvise
play music of various times and places	
perform in an ensemble	
In which areas will you commit yourself to becoming more independent?	

Get Acquainted with the Recorder

MAKE A SOUND!

- Blow into the mouthpiece of the recorder.
- Experiment with different ways of blowing to get a sound you like.

CONTROL THE AIR FLOW!

- Blow hard! Blow gently! Do you hear any difference?

THIS MAY HELP!

- Tuck your lower lip over your lower teeth.
- Now close your lips gently around the mouthpiece.
- Blow again! Does the tone sound any different to you now?

CHANGE PITCHES!

Experiment: Find a way to make a pattern of tones that go down and up.

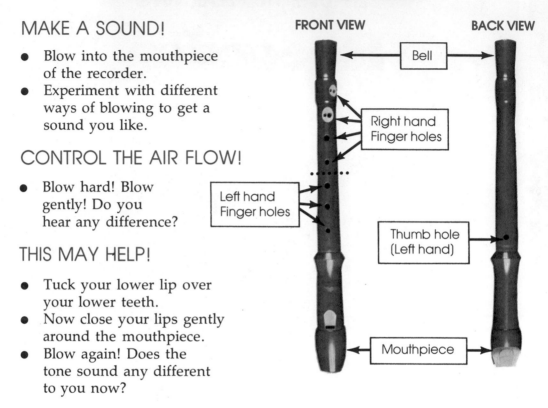

FRONT VIEW   BACK VIEW

Bell

Right hand Finger holes

Left hand Finger holes

Thumb hole (Left hand)

Mouthpiece

A COMPOSITION FOR RECORDER AND HAND PERCUSSION

- Plan and perform "A Composition for Recorder and Hand Percussion" using the sounds you have explored.
- Form small groups and choose a conductor.
- Your composition must be at least 15 seconds long.
- It must include silence and have a point of excitement.
- Invite your classmates to discuss your composition.
- Did your piece meet the musical requirements?

Hands On!

LEFT HAND:
- Cover the thumb hole with the pad of your thumb.
- Cover the second hole with the pad of your middle finger.

RIGHT HAND:
- Support the bell of the recorder. Be careful not to interfere with any holes.

LEFT HAND AGAIN:
- Lift your thumb off the thumb hole.

RIGHT HAND:
- Support the bell of the recorder as before.

Now using these two pitches on the recorder,

CREATE   an **introduction**   **interludes**   a **coda**

Accompany the singing on bells, xylophone, or piano:

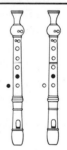

IF I SING AHEAD OF YOU

Traditional Round

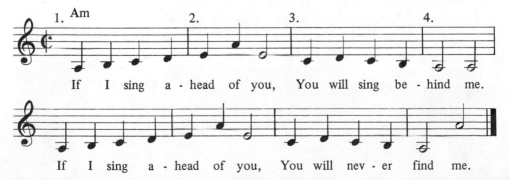

If I sing a - head of you, You will sing be - hind me.

If I sing a - head of you, You will nev - er find me.

Improving the Tone

- Hold the recorder in your hands as shown at the top of page 139.
- Place just the tip of the mouthpiece on your lower lip.
- Close your upper lip over the mouthpiece.

- **START** the sound with "duh" as you blow gently.
- **SUPPORT** the sound by controlling your breath as you do when singing.
- **END** the sound — bring your tongue up as though you were going to say "duh" again.

START ——————————→ SUPPORT ——————————→ END
"duh . . . . d"

Practice starting and stopping tones while you play several pitches on the recorder. Be sure that each hole is well covered. If you are covering the holes correctly, they will leave small circles on the pads of your fingers.

Play Melodies

- Discover how to play these three simple tunes on the recorder.
- Begin on the pitches that are shown.
- Start and stop each tone as you have practiced.

MARY HAD A LITTLE LAMB

RAIN, RAIN, GO AWAY

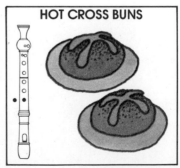
HOT CROSS BUNS

Play Folk Songs

First practice the fingerings you will need to play the recorder descant to this Newfoundland sea chantey. Decide who will sing and who will play the recorder. Then switch parts.

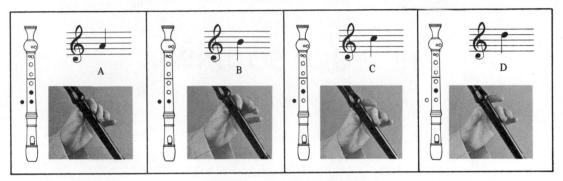

I'SE THE B'Y

Newfoundland Sea Chantey

I'se the b'y that builds the boat, and
I'se the b'y that sails her! I'se the b'y that
cat - ches the fish and takes them home to Li - zer.

Play "Hop Old Squirrel" and "Good News" on the recorder. These two songs use some of the pitches you have already learned, as well as a new one, G.

These songs use tones of shorter duration. Start each short tone by thinking "duh."

HOP OLD SQUIRREL

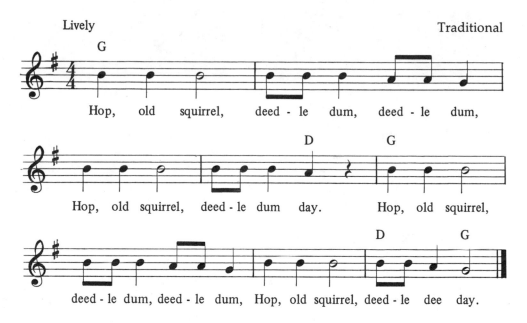

Lively   Traditional

Hop, old squirrel, deed-le dum, deed-le dum,

Hop, old squirrel, deed-le dum day. Hop, old squirrel,

deed-le dum, deed-le dum, Hop, old squirrel, deed-le dee day.

Create an ostinato pattern to accompany "Hop Old Squirrel." Use G, A, B, D, or E. Play the pattern on bells or xylophone.

GOOD NEWS

Spiritual

Good news! Cha-ri-ot's a-com-in'! Good

news! Cha - ri - ot's a - com - in'! Good news!

Cha - ri - ot's a - com-in', And I don'-na wan'-na be left be - hind.

Learn the fingerings for low E and F#.

High E uses the same fingering as low E except you cover only half the thumb hole!

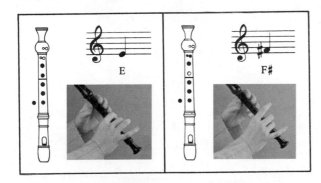

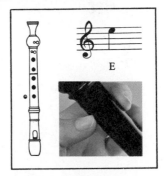

WE LIVE AT THE EDGE OF TOWN

Jewish Folk Song

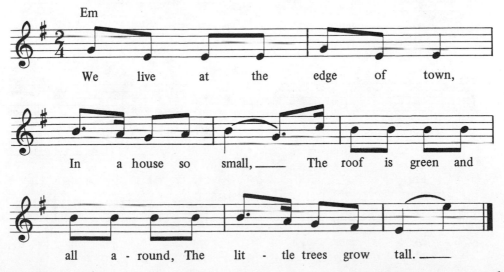

We live at the edge of town,

In a house so small,___ The roof is green and

all a - round, The lit - tle trees grow tall.___

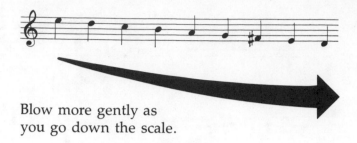

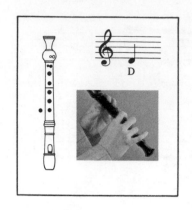

Blow more gently as
you go down the scale.

When you play low tones on the recorder,
be sure that the holes are firmly covered.

Play this repeated accompaniment pattern
on recorder or another instrument. Others
may sing or play the melody.

ARIRANG

Words Adapted

Korean Folk Song

1. A - ri - rang,— A - ri - rang,— A - ri - rang,— A - ri - rang,—
2. A - ri - rang,— A - ri - rang,— A - ri - rang,— A - ri - rang,—

A - ri - rang,— A - ri - rang,— A - ri - rang fair.
A - ri - rang,— A - ri - rang,— A - ri - rang fair.

Through the pass — I watch you go — there. _____
Here I wait for you, wait, wait and — stare. _____

A - ri - rang,— A - ri - rang,— A - ri - rang fair.
A - ri - rang,— A - ri - rang,— A - ri - rang fair.

144

Practice the fingerings for C and F. Then play "Wanderin'."

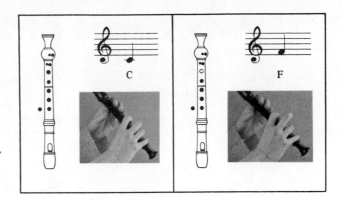

WANDERIN'

American Folk Song

I've been work-in' in the cit-y, I've been work-in' on the farm. But

all I've got to show for it is mus-cle in my arm, And it

looks like I'm nev-er gon-na cease my wan-der-in'.

A SONG-TO-BE

Anonymous

I wonder why
My song-to-be that I wish to use,
My song-to-be that I wish to put together,
I wonder why it will not come to me.

- Recorder performers play one pitch together.
- Breathe at different times to sustain the sound.
- At the same time, others may speak the poem.

Play Music of Today

Learn to play "Walkin' Blues" on your recorder. Remember . . . you must blow gently to produce the low tones.

WALKIN' BLUES

by B. A.

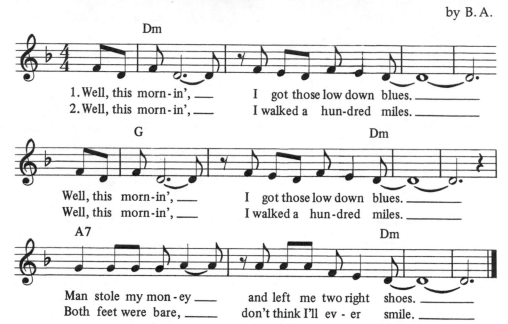

1. Well, this morn-in', ___   I   got those low down blues. _____
2. Well, this morn-in', ___   I walked a   hun-dred   miles. _____

Well, this   morn-in', ___   I   got those low down blues. _____
Well, this   morn-in', ___   I walked a   hun-dred   miles. _____

Man stole my mon-ey ___   and left me two right   shoes. _____
Both feet were bare, ___   don't think I'll ev-er   smile. _____

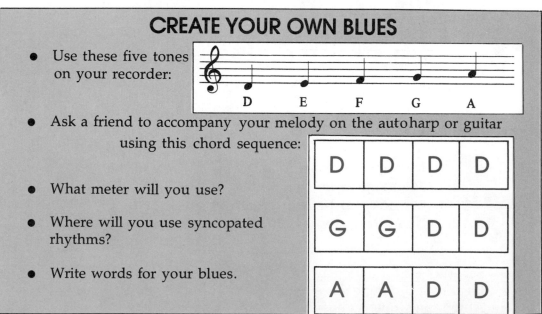

CREATE YOUR OWN BLUES

- Use these five tones on your recorder:

  D   E   F   G   A

- Ask a friend to accompany your melody on the autoharp or guitar using this chord sequence:

D	D	D	D
G	G	D	D
A	A	D	D

- What meter will you use?

- Where will you use syncopated rhythms?

- Write words for your blues.

146

NEW ORLEANS

by Frank J. Guida and Joseph R. Royster

Listen to this lively piece of American jazz. The solo flute is played by the jazz flutist Herbie Mann.

Notice that the percussion plays the shortest sounds:

Listen to the piece several times to get the "feel" of the rhythm. Then improvise rhythm patterns on the following pitches as you play along with the recording.

Wait for the five-measure introduction before beginning:

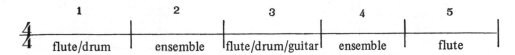

147

Play Music of Early Times

The recorder has been played for hundreds of years.

This old English folk song was probably played on the recorder.

Learn how to play the melody. Then ask some-one to accompany you by gently strumming the autoharp or guitar. Others may wish to sing.

Investiture of Saint Martin by Simone Martini (detail of musicians). San Francesco, Assisi. SCALA New York/Florence.

SCARBOROUGH FAIR

English Folk Song

Are you go-in' to Scar-bor-ough Fair? _____

Pars-ley, sage, rose-mar-y, and thyme; _____

Re-mem-ber me to one who lives there, _____ For

he / she once was a true love of mine. _____

148

In ancient times, small percussion instruments were often used to accompany the recorder. Create a light percussion accompaniment for this dance tune. Choose tambourines, drums, finger cymbals, or triangles. Then perform the piece in ensemble with some playing the recorders while others play percussion instruments.

ANCIENT DANCE

Old German Tune

MUSIC OF THE SPHERES

by Lord Byron

There's music in the singing of a reed;
There's music in the gushing of a rill;
There's music in all things, if men had ears;
The earth is but the music of the spheres.

- Form groups.
- Create a setting of this poem using recorders and percussion instruments.
- Choose a narrator to read the poem.
- Perform your composition for the class.

Listen to Music of Today

EONS AGO BLUES

by Robert Dorough

Although recorders are ancient instruments, they are still being used in today's music.

Listen to "Eons Ago Blues." It is performed on these five ancient instruments.

VIOLA DA GAMBA **RECORDERS**

SOPRANO ALTO TENOR BASS

Courtesy Pro Musica Antiqua

AS YOU LISTEN, DO YOU HEAR...

- echo and imitation between recorder parts?
- a wandering melodic line on alto recorder that establishes a feeling of blues?
- "close" harmonies that suggest the blues and jazz styles?
- the viola da gamba providing a walking bass to set the mood for the remainder of the piece?
- the easy blues rhythm?
- the recorders taking turns to embroider phrases?

150

Play Recorders in Ensemble

Learn to play this melody in unison on the recorder. Then divide the class into three groups and perform this song as a three-part canon.

TALLIS' CANON

Words by Thomas Ken

Music by Thomas Tallis

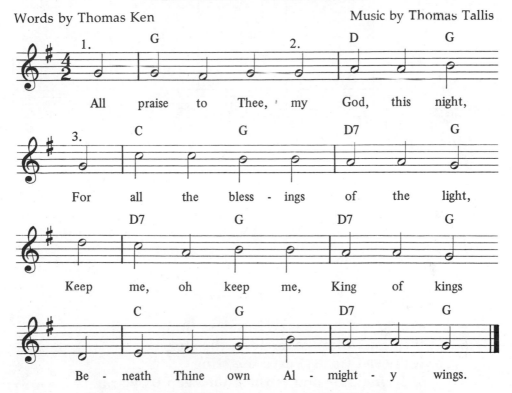

All praise to Thee, my God, this night,

For all the bless - ings of the light,

Keep me, oh keep me, King of kings

Be - neath Thine own Al - might - y wings.

IMPROVISE ON AN ANCIENT SCALE

MELODY Choose any of the tones of this ancient scale to create a melody on the recorder. You must begin and end on D.

D - Dorian

HARMONY Ask a friend to play a drone accompaniment for your tune:

Autoharp: Press the D Major and D Minor buttons at the same time. Strum rhythm patterns using 𝅗𝅥 or 𝅝 .

Piano: Use the sustaining (middle) peddle as you play this drone:

Use your recorder to perform music of many styles. Your book includes a variety of songs you will be able to play. Use the following chart as reference for some of the pitches you have not yet played.

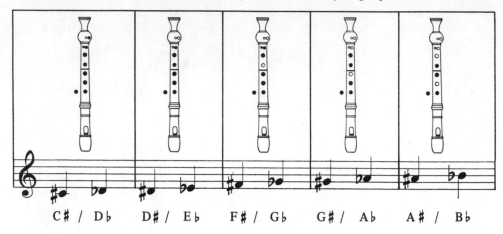

C♯ / D♭   D♯ / E♭   F♯ / G♭   G♯ / A♭   A♯ / B♭

SONNET

by Gene Lees

Music is a strange and useless thing.
It doesn't offer cover from the storm.
It doesn't (really) ease the sting
of living; nor nourish us, nor keep us warm.

And men expend their lives in search of sound,
learning how to juggle bits of noise,
and by their swift illusions to confound
the heart with fleeting and evasive joys.
Yet I am full of quaking gratitude
that this exalted folly still exists,

that in an age of cold computer mood,
a piper still can whistle in the mists.
His notes are pebbles falling into time.
How sweetly made it is, and how sublime.

SELF-DIRECTED LEARNING

Ukulele

YOUR COMMITMENT TO SELF-DIRECTED LEARNING

Which of these can you now do independently?	
tune the ukulele	accompany songs with accurate chords and rhythms
play chords in tune	read chord symbols and respond to musical notation
improvise chordal accompaniments and/or melodies	
In which areas will you commit yourself to becoming more independent?	

Get Acquainted with the Ukulele

1. Learn how to hold your ukulele:

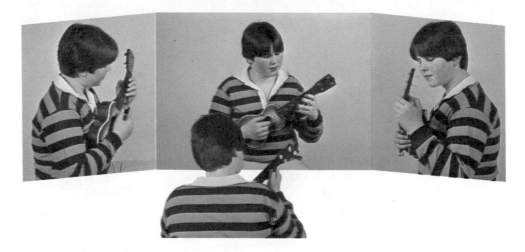

2. Find these parts:

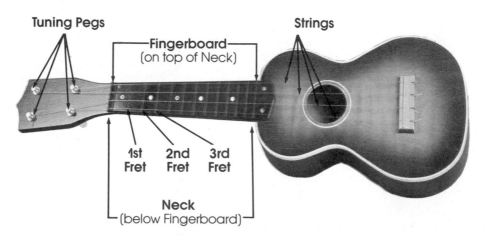

3. Now hold your ukulele in playing position.
   Count the strings.
   The string nearest the floor is String 1.
4. Count the frets.
   The fret nearest the tuning pegs is the 1st fret.

Left Hand Changes the Pitches

Hold the neck of the ukulele with your left hand as shown in Picture 1.

REMEMBER!

- Only the pad of your left thumb should touch the neck.
- Never let the neck rest on your left palm.

Experiment changing pitches. Press down on a string while plucking with the right hand. When you change finger positions, move the thumb along with the other fingers.

Right Hand Strums

Try these different ways of strumming:

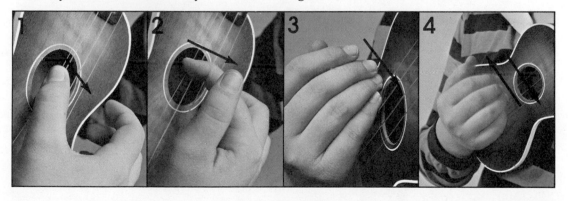

REMEMBER!

- Strumming is a wrist action. Move only your right hand and wrist, not your entire arm.

Read Chord Positions

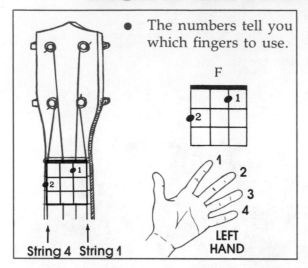

- The numbers tell you which fingers to use.

String 4   String 1

LEFT HAND

- Play the **F** chord while you sing this song.

Strum

$\frac{2}{4}$

- Begin to sing on this pitch:

GROUNDHOG

Arranged and adapted
by Buffy Sainte-Marie

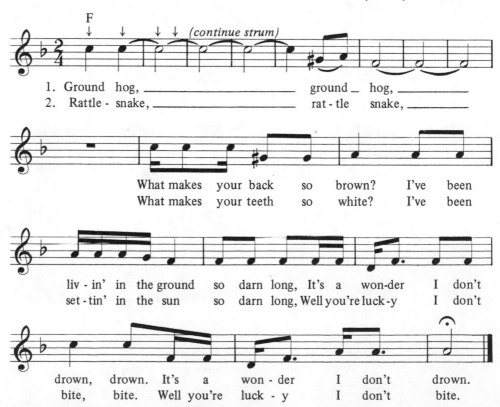

1. Ground hog, _____ ground _ hog, _____
2. Rattle - snake, _____ rat - tle snake, _____

What makes   your back   so   brown?   I've   been
What makes   your teeth   so   white?   I've   been

liv - in' in the ground   so darn long, It's a   won - der   I don't
set - tin' in the sun   so darn long, Well you're luck - y I don't

drown, drown. It's a   won - der   I don't   drown.
bite, bite. Well you're luck - y I don't   bite.

Tune Your Ukulele

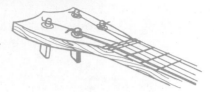

1. There is one peg for each string.
   - Find the peg that is attached to String 4.

2. Change the pitch of String 4.
   - Pluck it as you slowly turn its peg until you hear the string change pitch. How did the pitch change?
   - Now turn the peg in the opposite direction until you hear the pitch change again. How did the pitch change this time?

3. Tune String 4 to a specific pitch—G.
   - Use any of these methods to find the correct pitches for all four strings:

4. Ukulele strings quickly stretch out of tune. You will often need to retune your instrument between songs.

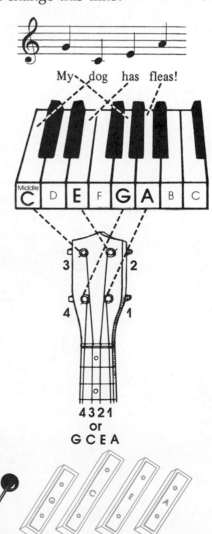

My dog has fleas!

Middle C D E F G A B C

3   2
4   1

4 3 2 1
or
G C E A

Songs for Recreation

You may know this melody by another name! Before you perform it, practice moving between the **F** and **C7** chords.

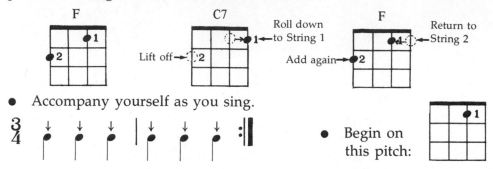

- Accompany yourself as you sing.

- Begin on this pitch:

FOUND A PEANUT

Nonsense Song

1. Found a pea - nut, found a pea - nut, Found a
2. It was rot - ten, it was rot - ten, It was
3. Ate it any - way, ate it any - way, Ate it

(continue strum)

pea - nut last ___ night. Last ___ night I found a
rot - ten last ___ night. Last ___ night ___ it was
any - way last ___ night. Last ___ night I ate it

pea - nut, Found a pea - nut last ___ night.
rot - ten, It was rot - ten last ___ night.
any - way, Ate it any - way last ___ night.

4. Got sick . . .   7. I died anyway . . .
5. Called the doctor . . . 8. Went to heaven . . .
6. Had an operation . . .   9. Woke up . . .

THE UPWARD TRAIL

- Beginning pitch:

Traditional

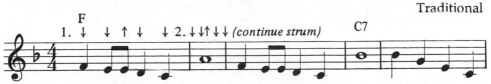

We're on the up-ward trail, We're on the up-ward trail, Sing-ing, sing-ing,

ev - 'ry-bod - y sing - ing, as we go. home - ward bound!

- Play the **C** chord to accompany this familiar song:

- Beginning pitch:

- Improvise a strumming pattern using downward and upward motions.

ROW, ROW, ROW YOUR BOAT

Traditional Round

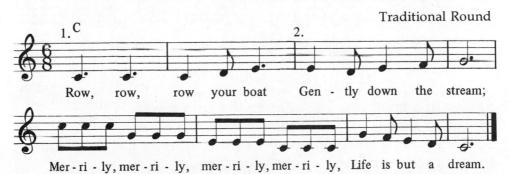

Row, row, row your boat Gen - tly down the stream;

Mer - ri - ly, mer - ri - ly, mer - ri - ly, mer - ri - ly, Life is but a dream.

Have some fun with this song. Upon each repetition of it, leave off the last word you sang the previous time. In this manner, you will "erase" the words so that only the accompaniment remains.

. . . Life is but a dream.   . . . Life is but a   . . . Life is but

More Songs for Recreation

Practice moving between the **C** and **G7** chords before you play and sing this song.

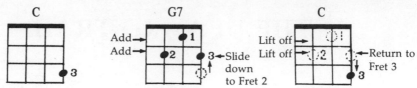

● Begin: open

THREW IT
OUT THE WINDOW

Nonsense Song

Lit-tle Jack Hor-ner sat in a cor-ner Eat-ing his Christ-mas pie. ___

He stuck in his thumb and pulled out a plum, And threw it out the win-dow! _

D. S. al Fine

The win-dow, _ the win-dow, _ He threw it out the win-dow. _

SPIDER

by B. A.

Spider in a cobweb,   I'm gonna spin a web
Spider in a tree,   Like a spider in a tree,
Spider comes a creepin'   Gonna catch a pretty gal (handsome guy)
But he can't catch me.   Just for me.

● Rhythmically chant the poem while you strum the **C** and **G7** chords.
● Begin and end on the **C** chord.
● Try changing chords where you think it is appropriate.
● When you are satisfied with your chord sequence, improvise a melody for the words.

Practice moving between these chords. You only need to learn one new chord, **C7**.

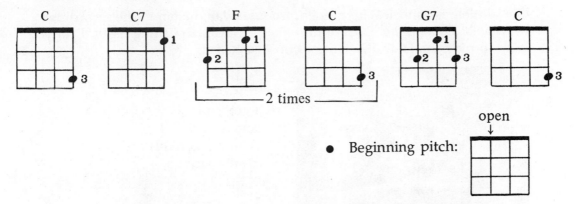

C   C7   F   C   G7   C

— 2 times —

● Beginning pitch: open

WHO'S GONNA SHOE YOUR PRETTY LITTLE FOOT?

American Folk Song

1. Who's gon - na shoe your pret - ty lit - tle foot,
2. Pa - pa's gon - na shoe my pret - ty lit - tle foot,

Who's gon - na glove ___ your hand, ___
Ma - ma's gon - na glove ___ my hand, ___ And

Who's gon - na kiss ___ your red ru - by lips,
sis - ter's gon - na kiss ___ my red ru - by lips,

Who's gon - na be your man? ___
I don't ___ need no man. ___

Sounds of Hawaiian Music

The ukulele is a musical instrument from Hawaii. Listen to the recording of "The Hukilau Song," which describes a Hawaiian fishing party. Learn how to play the Hawaiian Strum you just heard.

1. Cup your right hand just above String 4. Your fingernails are close to the strings.

2. Briskly open your hand, leading with Finger 4. The other three fingers follow in rapid succession. Make sure each finger brushes across all four strings from top to bottom. This will produce a "fluttering" sound.

3. Finger 1 (the index finger) provides the accent.

- Practice the Hawaiian Strum so that you can do it within the time span of a single beat:

  Fingers flutter → End with Finger 1   Fingers flutter → End with Finger 1

- Accompany "The Hukilau Song" with this pattern combining the Hawaiian Strum with down and up strokes:

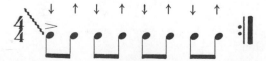

● Learn how to play the D chord.

● Beginning pitch: open

THE HUKILAU SONG

Words and music by Jack Owens

Oh, we're go - in' to the Hu - ki - lau, Hu - ki,

(continue strum)

Hu - ki, Hu - ki, Hu - ki, Hu - ki, Hu - ki - lau, Ev - 'ry -

bod - y loves the Hu - ki - lau, where the lau - lau is the kau - kau at the

Hu - ki - lau. Oh, we throw the net out

in - to the sea, ___ and all the a - ma a - ma come a -

swim - min' to me. ___ Oh, we're go - in' to the

Hu - ki - lau, Hu - ki, Hu - ki, Hu - ki, Hu - ki, Hu - ki - lau.

Old-Time Songs

- This song uses three chords you already know and introduces a new one, **D minor**.

Dm

- Beginning pitch:

- Improvise your own strum.

PUT YOUR ARMS AROUND ME HONEY

by Junie McCree and Albert Von Tilzer

Barred Chords

To play "Bill Bailey," you will need to learn two **barred chords.**

● Bar the **B♭** chord

First place Finger 1 of your left hand on Strings 1 and 2 on the first fret;

Then, place Finger 2 on String 3, second fret;

Finally, place Finger 3 on String 4, third fret.

● Bar the **D7** chord

Cover all the strings in the second fret with Finger 2;

Then, place Finger 3 on String 1, third fret.

BILL BAILEY

Words and Music by Hughie Cannon

Won't you come home, Bill Bai - ley, Won't you come home,

She cried the whole night long? _____ I'll do the

dish - es, hon - ey, I'll pay the rent. I know I

done you wrong. ____ 'Mem - ber that rain - y eve - ning

I drove you out With noth - in' but a fine - tooth comb? _

____ I know I'm to blame, Well, ___ ain't that a

shame, Bill Bai - ley, won't you please come home?

More Songs to Accompany

There are many songs in this book you will now be able to accompany on the ukulele. As you sing and play these songs, experiment with different strumming styles.

- **THE COWBOY,** page 36   Key: **F major**

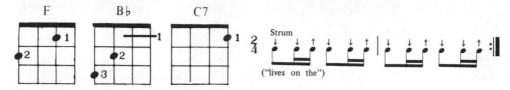

("lives on the")

- **TZENA, TZENA,** page 92   Key: **C major**

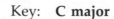
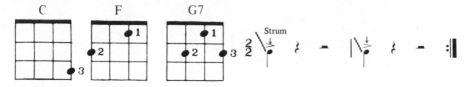

- **TRINIDAD,** page 184   Key: **G major**

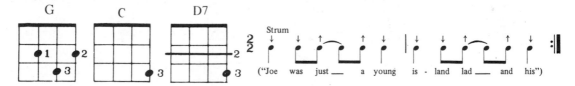

("Joe was just — a young is-land lad — and his")

- **EVERYBODY LOVES SATURDAY NIGHT,** page 44

                                        Key: **D major**

- **TUM BALALYKA,** page 124   Key: **D minor**

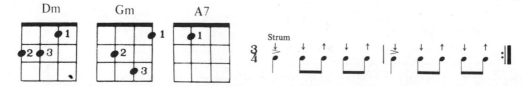

Can you find other songs to accompany?

The Instrumental Ensemble

Which role will you play
in the musical ensemble?

How sensitive can you be
to the needs of
the group as a whole?

YOUR COMMITMENT TO LEARNING

Which of these can you now do independently?		
perform in an instrumental ensemble	arrange your own instrumental ensemble music	describe differences in ensemble music of different styles
experiment with musical controls to develop expressive performances		compose music in a specific style
In which areas will you commit yourself to becoming more independent?		

Planning an Ensemble Arrangement

To find out what kinds of musical decisions are made when building an arrangement, listen to The Burly Five as they develop a Dixieland jazz arrangement of "When the Saints Go Marching In."

Start with a favorite tune.

Oh, when the Saints _____ go march - ing in, _____

Oh, when the Saints go _____ march - ing in, _____

Oh, Lord, I _____ want to be in that num - ber _____

When the Saints go march - ing in. _____

Decide on an instrumentation typical of the musical style.

In Dixieland jazz, the rhythm section generally stresses the basic beat, but the snare drum provides accents on "off-beats."

Add the melody.

The trumpeter takes the lead, "decorating" the melody with "extra tones," and syncopating the rhythm.

Provide a harmonic accompaniment.

The trombone adds interest by playing patterns made up of chordal tones and stepwise passages.

The clarinet also adds harmonic interest, playing a countermelody that moves with mostly short tones. Notice that this part also uses chordal tones, "tied together" with passing tones and neighboring tones.

Now listen to the complete arrangement of "When the Saints Go Marching In." It reflects many of the characteristics of early Dixieland style.

WORRIED MAN

American Folk Song

It takes a wor-ried man to sing a wor-ried song. It

takes a wor-ried man to sing a wor-ried song. It

takes a wor-ried man to sing a wor-ried song. I'm wor-ried

now _____ but I won't be wor-ried long.

Try creating your own Dixieland arrangement of this familiar song. Use ideas from the recording of "When the Saints Go Marching In."

INSTRUMENTATION: If the instruments you heard are not available, what might you substitute? You need at least one "lead" melody player, one or two instruments to play the bass line, an instrument to play a high counter-melody, and drums.

RHYTHM SECTION: Build on the ideas you heard in "When the Saints Go Marching In." Which beats will you stress?

MELODY LEAD: Find places in the melody to add "extra tones." Can you change the rhythm to make the song more syncopated?

172

HARMONIC ACCOMPANIMENT: Here are the three chords you need to accompany this song. They are written for bass instruments.

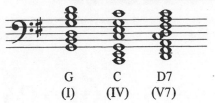

Choose tones from these chords to provide the bass line and harmony part. "Walk" from one tone to the next to add interest.

Be sure to play chordal tones on accented beats. Listen carefully to know when to change chords.

COUNTERMELODY: The high-pitched instrument may use tones from these same three chords. Make up a countermelody, using chordal tones and passing tones that move with the short sound.

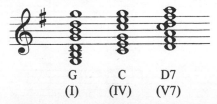

173

ACCOMPANY YOUR FRIENDS

GHOST OF TOM

Traditional Round

Choose some people to sing the round.

Have you seen the ghost of Tom? Long white bones with the

flesh all gone. _____ Oh, _____

Would-n't it be chill-y with no skin on?

Then add these harmonic **ostinatos.** Each pattern is repeated over and over to provide an accompaniment.

ALTO XYLOPHONE
Right Hand

Left Hand

ALTO METALLOPHONE

SOPRANO XYLPHONE

glissando

ALTO GLOCKENSPIEL

Plan interludes of "weird" sounds between repetitions of the melody. Use slide whistle, tambourine, temple blocks, cowbell.

Review the melody of "Ev'ry Night When the Sun Goes In," pages 94–95. Then plan an accompaniment using any or all of the following patterns.

Will you use the same combination of patterns throughout?

Some people may want to add the vocal **ostinatos** on page 95 for a complete arrangement.

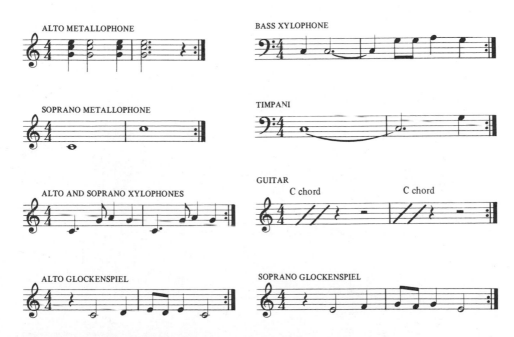

Plan interludes between the verses. Continue playing the instrumental ostinatos for several measures while one person adds vocal improvisation. Before you begin the interlude, decide how many measures the improvisation should last.

Changing Styles

Arranged by Buryl Red

By changing the instrumentation, the rhythm, or the arrangement of the harmony parts, you can change the style of a song.

Follow the suggestions given below to make a "country" arrangement of "He's Got the Whole World in His Hands."

RHYTHM SECTION: Drums play a steady beat, accenting beats two and four. Play chords in this rhythm on autoharp or guitar.

VOCAL PARTS: Country vocalists usually add a harmonizing part above the melody.

HARMONY: Play "fills" on piano wherever you see a half note.

for C chords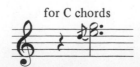

for G7 chords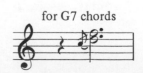

Expressive Singing

HE'S GOT THE WHOLE WORLD
IN HIS HANDS

Preparing a musical performance requires more than assigning parts and turning the notes into sound. It is the responsibility of each performer to help the composer's ideas "come alive" by communicating them as musically as possible.

Listen to two performances of "He's Got the Whole World in His Hands." The first is by Odetta, a great Black-American folk singer. The second is by Leontyne Price, a great Black-American opera singer.

The music is the same in both performances. Have both performers communicated the same meaning? Discuss reasons for your answers by comparing the ways the two performers shape individual phrases, as well as the complete songs.

Note differences in the ways each artist uses these musical controls to "mold" an expressive musical line.

TEMPO   DYNAMICS   TONE QUALITY
        ACCENT   ARTICULATION

Can you describe the changes you hear? What about phrasing? Does the artist perform each musical idea as a single thought, or as a series of fragments?

As you rehearse your vocal performance, experiment with different ways of using these musical controls. Experiment until you feel that your performances express the musical and verbal ideas of the composition.

Country Music

RED RIVER VALLEY

American Folk Song

"Red River Valley" is a typical country song. The music is the same for verse and refrain. It is harmonized with only three chords.

Listen to the recording. The arrangement is in traditional "bluegrass" style, with five-string banjo, fiddle, harmonica, guitar, string bass, and jaw harp.

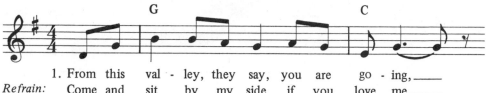

1. From this val - ley, they say, you are go - ing, ____
Refrain: Come and sit by my side if you love me, ____
2. Won't you think of the val - ley you're leav - ing? ____

We will miss your bright eyes and sweet smile,
Do not has - ten to bid me a - dieu,
Oh, how lone - ly, how sad it will be.

For they say you are tak - ing the sun - shine
But re - mem - ber the Red Riv - er val - ley
Oh ____ think of the fond heart you're break - ing

That ____ bright - ens our path - way a - while. ____
And the girl that has loved you so true. ____
And the grief you are giv - ing to me. ____

178

Modern country music combines many different popular styles. For example, The Eagles, Fleetwood Mac, James Taylor, and Linda Ronstadt are known mainly as rock musicians, but can also be called country artists. Freddy Fender and Johnny Rodriguez represent Latin influences on country music. Even singers from other countries, such as Gordon Lightfoot and Olivia Newton-John, are considered to be country artists.

Today, a single country tune can be sung in different ways by different people and still be identified as "country music."

Your Own Progressive-Country Arrangement

Compare this version of "Red River Valley" with the original country song. What differences do you notice in melody, rhythm, harmony?

As you plan your progressive-country arrangement:
- Add heavy accents in the rhythm section. Emphasize the third beat of each measure.
- Establish a steady pattern of short sounds on tambourine.
- Play chord patterns on autoharp or guitar in the same rhythm as the tambourine part.
- Play chord roots on cello or bass in this rhythm.

179

Your Own Country-Gospel Arrangement

How does this arrangement differ from the progressive-country version? Describe changes in melody, rhythm, and harmony.

ACCOMPANIMENT: Play chord roots on bass in this rhythm.

Play chords on autoharp or guitar in this rhythm.

Slap a tambourine in this rhythm.

© John Reggero 1978

Probably the most important example of the influence of country music was Elvis Presley. Presley started as a country singer, fusing country music with elements of gospel and rhythm-and-blues, and developed a style that earned him the title of "king of rock-and-roll."

180

COMPOSE YOUR OWN COUNTRY WALTZ

Many country lyrics deal with events of everyday life. A common expression, such as "better late than never," often serves as the main idea.

The main idea, combined with its melody, is known as the "hook" because it "hooks" the listener into liking the song!

Compose your own country waltz, using the phrase "better late than never" as the hook. First, finish the lyrics for the refrain.

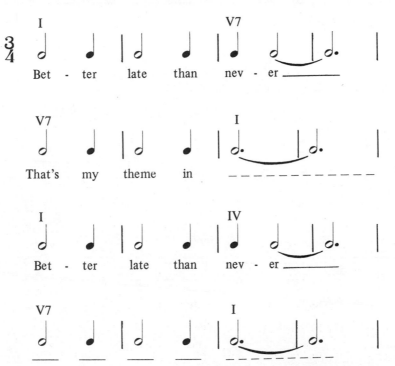

Now write one or two verses that apply this phrase to your own life.

Use the same chord progression in the verse, but make the melody of the verse simpler.

When your song is complete, add an accompaniment. Use ideas from "Your Own Bluegrass Arrangement," pages 22–23. Or create new accompaniment ideas.

BOUND FOR THE PROMISED LAND

American Folk Hymn
Arranged by Buryl Red

With a flowing feeling

On Jor - dan's storm - y banks I stand And cast a

wish - ful eye; To _____ Ca - naan's _____ fair and

hap - py __ land Where __ my pos - ses - sions lie.

Bound for the land _____ I'm

I am bound for the prom - ised land, _____ I'm

bound for the land: Oh, _____ who will come and

bound for the prom - ised land; Oh, _____ who will __ come and

go __ with __ me, I am bound prom - ised land. _____

go __ with __ me, I am bound for the prom - ised land. _____

"Folk-rock" combines the sounds of country with the sounds of rock.

Compare this version of "Bound for the Promised Land" with the one on page 120. Notice the differences in key and meter.

Prepare a folk-rock performance of this song using the patterns below.

RHYTHM: Choose from these patterns.

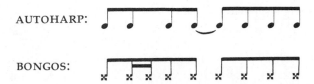

MELODY: Will you sing with the same vocal quality you used for the rock version of "Red River Valley"?

HARMONY: The low voices may add a harmonizing part during the second phrase.

High voices take over the harmony during the last two phrases.

Use cello or another stringed instrument. Choose from the pitches shown below for the appropriate chords.

Now listen to a "gospel" version of this song. In what ways have melody and rhythm been altered?

Compare this recording with a "soul" version of "He's Got the Whole World in His Hands." What similarities and differences do you notice? Can you create an arrangement of a song you know in one of these styles?

Go Calypso!

TRINIDAD

Words and Music
by Massie Patterson and Sammy Heyward

1. Joe was just __ a young is - land lad, __ and his
2. Joe, he bought __ all her wed - ding clothes, __ but this
3. Trin - i - dad, __ she was ver - y cute, __ and they

girl friend named __ Trin - i - dad, She would not an - swer a
was the start __ of his woes; He bought a dress __ made of
said she was __ quite a beaut, But she said she __ did not

yes or no, __ this young girl from Puer - to Ri - co.
fine sat - in, __ but now where's the love - ly Lat - in?
care to wed, __ her heart was in San __ Juan in - stead.

Refrain

Trin - i - dad, __ oh Trin - i - dad, __ please, my dar - ling, don't

act so mean, __ Please come back __ to me,

ain't it plain __ to see, I will make __ you my queen.

Add your own calypso accompaniment to "Trinidad."

RHYTHM: Choose from these traditional calypso patterns.

HARMONY: Play chords on xylophone, autoharp, or guitar in rhythms
such as the following.

MELODY: To suggest the sound of steel drums, play the melody on metallophone or bells.

Try plucking melodic tones as you strum the chords.

Music for Steel Band

YELLOW BIRD

Listen to "Yellow Bird" played by a steel band from the Caribbean. Notice the rhythmic accompaniment, typical of calypso music, played on drums, cymbals, and cowbells.

You can make your own steel drums.

1. Collect some one-gallon cans. Gently punch the end of each can into a concave shape with a ¾" dowel stick and a mallet.
2. Turn the can over and set it on the open end of another can approximately the size of a frozen juice can. Place this can to one side of the depressed end.
3. Tap from the inside of the larger can and gradually make a small depression over the smaller can. Test this "bubble" for its pitch by turning over the can and tapping it.
4. Use a second open-ended can, one slightly larger than the juice can, to make another bubble. The pitch of this bubble should be slightly lower. Test it as you make it.
5. You may use cans of other sizes to produce more "steel drums." See how many different pitches you can make. Paint the name of the pitch on the bubble. Use these cans separately, or join them to form a larger steel drum. Experiment with a variety of mallets to produce a desirable sound.

COMPOSE YOUR OWN CALYPSO

Dennis Stock/Magnum

A calypso singer
often invents lyrics
"on the spot" that

- tell of a recent event.
- describe an important person.
- express the mood of the moment.

All day, all night, I cry and moan,
Why, mom, oh why can't I stay home?
I'm much too sick to go to school,
?   ?   ?   ?   ? ? ?   ?

Tap a series of short sounds.
Then develop a syncopated rhythm for your lyrics.

NOT

Plan a chord sequence. A typical one will use only two chords in a
sequence such as:

I	I	I	V7
V7	V7	V7	I
I	I	I	V7
V7	V7	V7	I

Choose a key (such as C). Locate the chords on autoharp or ukulele.
Strum the chords as you improvise the melody.
Calypso tunes often move by skips, outlining the underlying chords.

Finally, add an accompaniment that includes a calypso rhythm section.
Follow the suggestions on page 185.

Your Own
Latin-Pop Arrangement

Like country music, modern Latin American music combines many popular musical styles. Each Latin American country and Caribbean island has its own music with its own distinct flavor.

Listen to "Chiapanecas," a Mexican folk song. The version you hear is in a different key from the one you see. Can you identify other differences between what you hear and what you see?

CHIAPANECAS

Mexican Folk Song

There's a song they know_ down in Mex - i - co; ___ Ev - 'ry

one seems_ to sing Chia - pa - ne - cas. ___ It's an

eas - y ___ thing, ___ once you feel the _ swing; ___ Sim - ply

let your - self go, Chia - pa - ne - cas. ___ Now then

sing a - long __ with this hap - py __ song, __ And you'll

soon feel __ the hol - i - day spir - it! _____ Join us

as we go __ to old Mex - i - co, __ And en -

joy the __ fi - es - ta __ *O - lé!* _____

So sing Chia - pa - ne - cas, *O - lé,*
Join in the fun, sing *O - lé,* } *O - lé,*

Say Chia - pa - ne - cas, *O - lé,* *O - lé!*

Dance, dance, ev - 'ry - one's danc - ing; Sing, sing,
dance, dance, join in the danc - ing; Mex - i -

ev - 'ry - one's sing - ing; Sway, sway, ev - 'ry - one's_
co's for ro - manc - ing; Come now, let your - self

_ feel - ing gay! _____ Come a - long now and
go and _

sing Chia - pa - ne - cas, *O - lé,* *O - lé!*

After you've learned the melody of "Chiapanecas," try combining some of the ideas shown on this page and the next. Develop your own "Latin-Pop" arrangement.

MELODY: Perform the melody in thirds to add a Mexican flavor. You might sing the melody and add the harmony part on bells, piano, clarinet, or violin.

RHYTHM: Establish a steady pattern of short sounds on maracas, bongos, or conga.

Play this pattern on guiro, maracas, or conga.

Play chord tones in this rhythm on steel drums.

HARMONY: Strum chords in steady eighth-notes on guitar or autoharp.
For a Spanish-guitar effect, pluck this pattern.

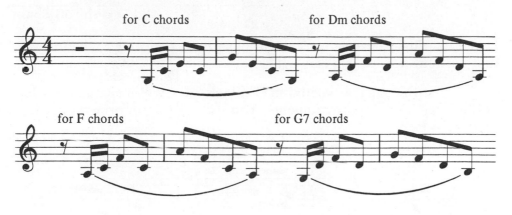

Pluck this Caribbean reggae pattern on cello or bass.

Play this countermelody on bells, recorder, or violin.

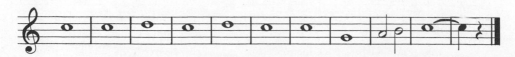

GREENSLEEVES

Old English Folk Song

Listen to "Greensleeves" as it might have been performed when it was first written, nearly 500 years ago.

Notice that the song is notated in D minor. This will make it easier for you to play it on your instruments. You will hear it performed one step higher, in E minor.

1. A - las! my love,__ you do me wrong,__ To
2. Ah, Green - sleeves, now__ fare - well, a - dieu,__ To

cast me off__ dis - cour - teous - ly; For I have loved __ you,
God I pray__ to pros - per thee, For I am still __ thy

oh, so long,__ De - light - ing in ___ your com - pa - ny.
sweet - heart true;__ Come once__ a - gain__ to meet me.

Refrain:

Green - sleeves __ was all my joy, __ And oh, Green - sleeves __ was

my de - light, Green - sleeves,__ my heart of gold,__ And

all _____ for La - dy Green - sleeves.

Perform "Greensleeves" as it might have been arranged when it was first written.

INSTRUMENTATION: On the recording, you hear voices, recorder, lute, and viola da gamba. Although you will not have all these instruments in your classroom, you can make substitutions that will sound "close."

For lute: autoharp, ukulele, or guitar
For viola da gamba: cello, or low strings of viola, guitar, or autoharp

RHYTHM: Pluck or bow the root of each chord on your low stringed instrument.

MELODY: Use a small vocal group. For added richness, learn this version of the melody on recorder. The ends of phrases are changed where the melody dips too low for the recorder.

to cast me off _____ dis - cour - teous - ly;

De - light - ing in your com - pa - ny

HARMONY: Strum arpeggios on autoharp, ukulele, or guitar.

Greensleeves
in Modern Dress

Arranged by Buryl Red

Perform a "1960's-rock" version of "Greensleeves." Listen to a recording session in which a rock combo develops this arrangement.

Use some of the ideas on the recording for your own arrangement.

Change the meter.

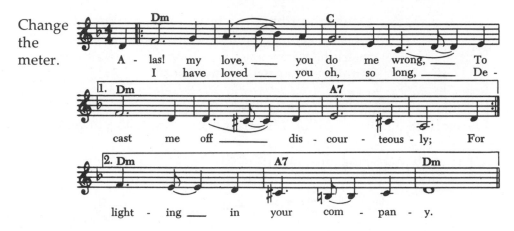

A - las! my love, ___ you do me wrong, ___ To
I have loved ___ you oh, so long, ___ De -

cast me off ___ dis - cour - teous - ly; For

light - ing ___ in your com - pan - y.

RHYTHM: Review some of the rhythmic patterns on page 51, "The Set Drummer." Play them now on drums or other percussion instruments.

HARMONY: Add vocal "fills" during the long tones in the melody.

Green - sleeves ___ was all my

BAH BAH BAH BAH BAH etc.

joy ___ And oh, Green - sleeves ___ was

Cello or bass might start with a simple bass line.

Then add extra tones as the chords change.

"Flesh out" the harmony on any keyboard or mallet instrument.

Or improvise a countermelody on bells or keyboard.

Expressive Playing

FANTASIA ON "GREENSLEEVES"

by Ralph Vaughan Williams

GREENSLEEVES

by The Ramsey Lewis Trio

When you play an instrument, you must make the same kinds of musical decisions as when you sing. You must decide how you are going to "shape" each musical phrase through changes in

TEMPO   DYNAMICS   TONE QUALITY
ACCENT   ARTICULATION

Listen to "Greensleeves" in a setting for string orchestra. Notice how the instrumentalists play this melody in a simple "singing" style. As you listen, determine where each phrase reaches its high point.

How do the performers use different musical controls to shape the phrases?

Compare this setting with an interpretation of the same melody by a jazz group. What differences do you notice in the way the phrases are shaped?

Return to the original "Greensleeves" melody. Sing or play it again. This time, try different ways of shaping the phrases.

Can you be as musical as the instrumentalists on the recordings?

The Musician at Work in a Recording Studio

When you listened to the recording session of the rock version of "Greensleeves" (page 196), you heard the producer and the performers working together to develop the final arrangement.

For this recording, the producer, Buryl Red, was also the arranger. His contributions, as well as those of the performers, are essential to the production of a recording such as this one.

But the performers and arranger cannot produce a recording by themselves. There are many other individuals who make equally important contributions to the final product.

HRW Photo by Ken Karp

THE STUDIO ENGINEER operates all of the recording equipment and is responsible for producing the actual tape. He or she sets up the tapes, adjusts levels of sounds, and offers suggestions for any special sound effects that may be required.

THE TAPE LIBRARIAN is responsible for storing the tapes. This person must maintain a system that makes it possible to quickly locate any tape that may be requested.

THE TAPE EDITOR is in charge of splicing (cutting) the tape of the final performance. If there is more than one track, the tape editor mixes the tracks and adjusts sound levels. For example, on the recording of "Greensleeves," the vocal track was recorded later and the tape editor mixed it in.

COMPOSE YOUR OWN 12-BAR BLUES

Twelve-bar blues is a truly American form. You can find examples of it in country music and rock music, as well as in other popular styles. Try composing your own 12-bar blues.

Begin by "talking" the blues:

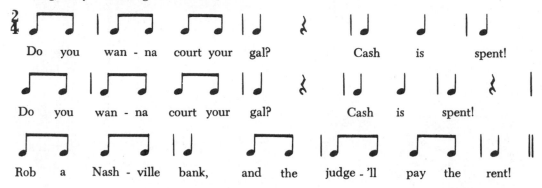

Do you wan-na court your gal?   Cash   is   spent!

Do you wan-na court your gal?   Cash   is   spent!

Rob   a   Nash-ville bank,   and   the   judge-'ll   pay   the   rent!

In many blues verses, such as the one above, the first two lines are the same. The third line is a "surprise statement."
Try writing words for your own blues verse.

Blues harmony

There are twelve bars (measures) in these blues. Play the chord sequence outlined below. Use autoharp, guitar, or piano as you "talk" the blues.

First four bars—play the C chord:

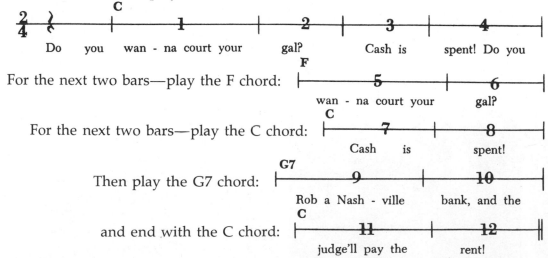

Do you wan-na court your   gal?   Cash is   spent! Do you

For the next two bars—play the F chord:

wan-na court your   gal?

For the next two bars—play the C chord:

Cash   is   spent!

Then play the G7 chord:

Rob a Nash-ville   bank, and the

and end with the C chord:

judge'll pay the   rent!

Now try the same sequence of chords with your own blues verse.

Blues melody

A blues melody is based on the major scale, but two tones—the third and seventh—are often lowered.

Major scale

Major scale with flat third and seventh

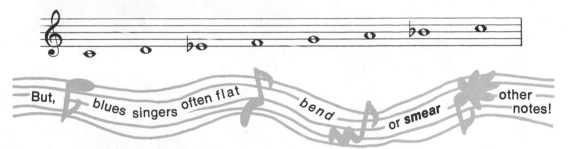

But, blues singers often flat bend or smear other notes!

These "flatted" tones sounding with the "non-flatted" tones in the harmony create **tension** in the blues.

Try making up a blues melody. Sing it, or play it on bells or piano.

Choose from these tones: Bars 1–4

Bars 5–6

Bars 7–8

Bars 9–10

Bars 11–12

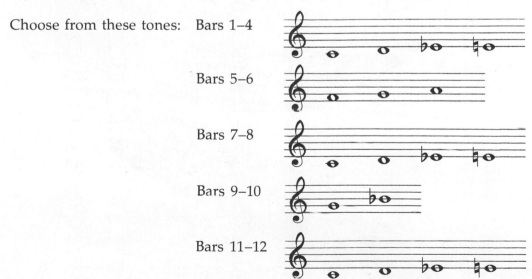

Put it together and add chords. Do you hear tension in your melody?

Now make up a melody for your own blues verse.

Erich Hartmann/Magnum

Unit V

THE CHORAL ENSEMBLE

You have a shouting voice. . . . .   a whispering voice. . . . . .
and several different speaking voices:

- for conversation
- for giving speeches
- for giving orders

Your singing voice can also be used in many different ways:

- rounds and canons
- descants and harmonies
- choral music

THE INDEPENDENT MUSICIAN

Which of these can you now do independently?			
produce "bright" and "dark" vocal sounds	use breath control for musical phrasing	use good diction to articulate song lyrics	sing in tune with others
In which areas will you commit yourself to becoming more independent?			

WONDERFUL COPENHAGEN

Words and Music by
Frank Loesser
Arranged by William Stickles

Won - der - ful, won - der - ful Co - pen - ha - gen,

Won - der - ful, won - der - ful Co - pen - ha - gen,

friend - ly old girl of a town, _____ With her

friend - ly old girl of a town, _____

har - bor light, that she wears at night, Like a

Like a

gold - en, gold - en crown. _____ Oh,

gold - en, gold - en crown. _____ Oh,

Learn to Use Your Singing Voice

You can control the kind of sound you make when you sing. This control is called **voice placement**.

Do this to practice singing with a "bright" sound. Hold your hand to the bridge of your nose.

Sing this.

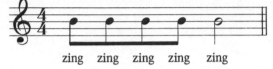

zing   zing   zing   zing   zing

Can you feel the vibrations in your nose? Now sing this.

zing   zing   zing   zing   zing   zing   zing   zing   zing   zing   *etc.*

Do this to practice singing with a "dark" sound.

Imagine that you are holding a hot potato in the back of your mouth. This will help you to open your throat. Now sing this.

hum _____   hum _____

SOMETIMES I FEEL LIKE A MOTHERLESS CHILD

American Folk Song
Arranged by Buryl A. Red

Practice singing this song with a dark sound.

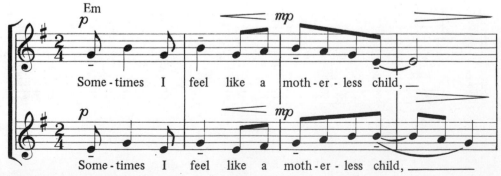

Some-times   I   feel   like   a   moth-er-less   child, ___

Some-times   I   feel   like   a   moth-er-less   child, ___

YOU'RE A GRAND OLD FLAG

Words and Music by George M. Cohan

You're a grand old flag, you're a high-fly-ing flag;

And for-ev-er in peace may you wave;____

You're the em-blem of the land I love,

The home of the free and the brave.____

Ev-ery heart beats true un-der red, white, and blue,

Where there's nev-er a boast or brag;____

But should auld ac-quaint-ance be for-got,

Keep your eye on the grand old flag.____

Use what you learned about voice placement to imitate instrumental sounds with the song "You're a Grand Old Flag." Sing the descant given below in the following ways:

1. Use a bright sound, like trumpets.

Ta ta ta ta ta

Use short, or **staccato, articulation.** Articulation is the way you start and stop each note.

2. Use a heavier, dark sound, to imitate French horns and tubas.

Bah bah bah bah bah

Use smooth, or **legato,** articulation.

3. What kind of articulation will you use to sound like flutes?

Loo loo loo loo loo

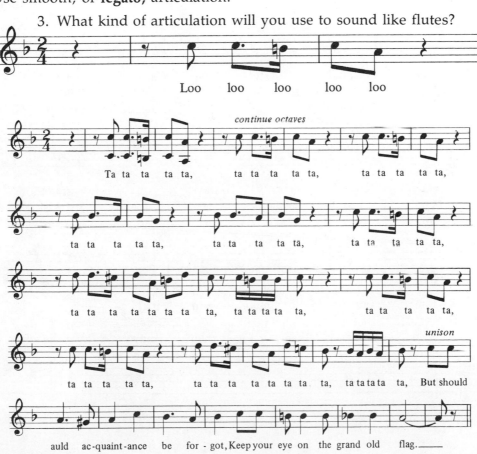

continue octaves

Ta ta ta ta ta,   ta ta ta ta ta,   ta ta ta ta ta,

ta ta ta ta ta,   ta ta ta ta ta,   ta ta ta ta ta,

ta ta ta ta ta ta ta, ta ta ta ta ta,   ta ta ta ta ta,

unison

ta ta ta ta ta,   ta ta ta ta ta ta ta, ta ta ta ta ta, But should

auld ac-quaint-ance be for-got, Keep your eye on the grand old flag.____

AMERICA, THE BEAUTIFUL

Words by Katharine Lee Bates　　　　　　　　Music by Samuel A. Ward

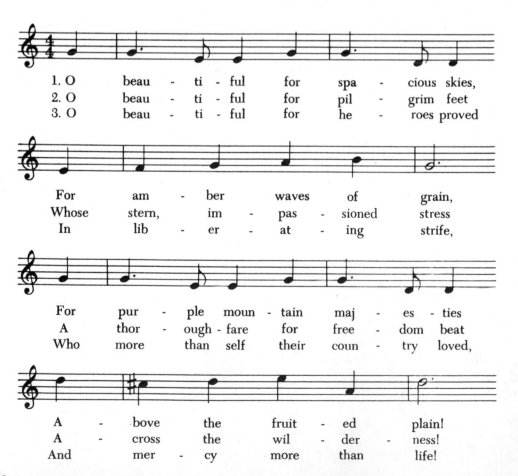

1. O beau - ti - ful for spa - cious skies,
2. O beau - ti - ful for pil - grim feet
3. O beau - ti - ful for he - roes proved

For am - ber waves of grain,
Whose stern, im - pas - sioned stress
In lib - er - at - ing strife,

For pur - ple moun - tain maj - es - ties
A thor - ough - fare for free - dom beat
Who more than self their coun - try loved,

A - bove the fruit - ed plain!
A - cross the wil - der - ness!
And mer - cy more than life!

A - mer - i - ca,   A - mer - i - ca,
A - mer - i - ca,   A - mer - i - ca,
A - mer - i - ca,   A - mer - i - ca,

God   shed   his   grace   on   thee,
God   mend   thine   ev - ery   flaw,
May   God   thy   gold   re - fine,

And   crown   thy   good   with   broth - er - hood
Con - firm   thy   soul   in   self - con - trol,
Till   all   suc - cess   be   no - ble - ness,

From   sea   to   shin - ing   sea.
Thy   lib - er - ty   in   law.
And   ev - ery   gain   di - vine.

Sing this descant with the refrain. What kind of articulation will you use?

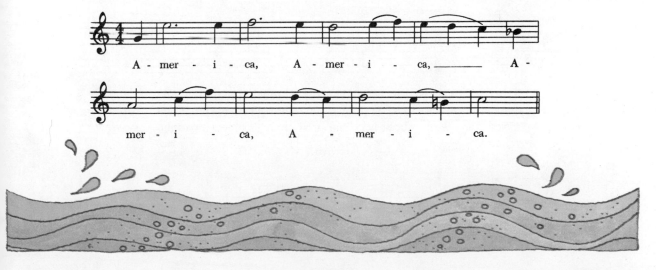

A - mer - i - ca,   A - mer - i - ca, _____   A -

mer - i - ca,   A - mer - i - ca.

COCKLES AND MUSSELS

Irish Folk Song

Will you use a bright or dark vocal sound to make the harmony part sound like the ghost of Molly Malone?

Liltingly

1. In Dub - lin's fair cit - y, where girls are so pret - ty,
2. She was a fish - mon-ger, but sure 'twas no won-der,
3. She died of a fe - ver and no one could save her,

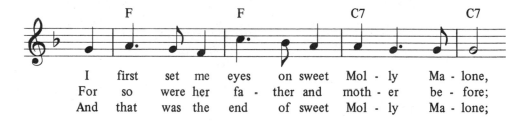

I first set me eyes on sweet Mol - ly Ma - lone,
For so were her fa - ther and moth - er be - fore;
And that was the end of sweet Mol - ly Ma - lone;

As she wheeled her wheel - bar - row through streets broad and nar - row,
And they wheeled their wheel - bar - row through streets broad and nar - row,
Now her ghost wheels her bar - row through streets broad and nar - row,

Cry - ing, "Cock-les and mus-sels, a - live, a - live oh!"

When you are reading music for chorus, you will sometimes see pitches written on the bass clef. The bass clef is used for pitches that are lower than those written on the treble clef. The pitches of both clefs meet at "middle C."

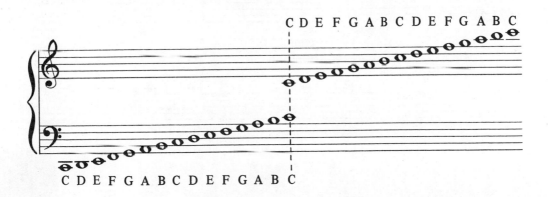

Which three pitches are used for the harmony part of "Cockles and Mussels"?

MINKA

English words by W. S. Haynie

Russian Folk Song

1. Min - ka, Min - ka, when I leave thee, How my sad heart
2. When I hear sweet mu - sic play - ing, Ev - ery note to

1. Min - ka, Min - ka, when I
2. When I hear sweet mu - sic

al - ways grieves me. When I'm gone I long to be with
me is say - ing, Min - ka, Min - ka, fair - est maid - en,

leave thee, How my sad heart
play - ing, Ev - ery note to

Min - ka, Min - ka mine. When I
Min - ka, Min - ka mine. When the

(Melody)

al - ways grieves me. When I see the
me is say - ing: When the win - ter

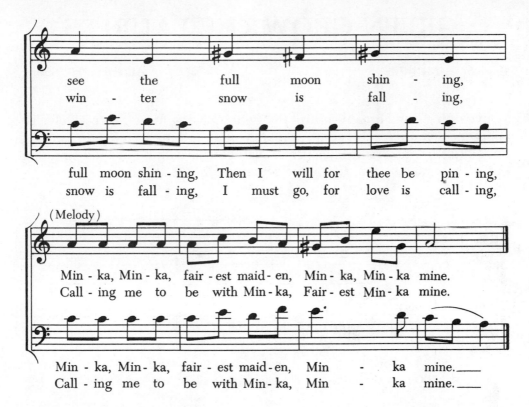

see the full moon shin - ing,
win - ter snow is fall - ing,

full moon shin - ing, Then I will for thee be pin - ing,
snow is fall - ing, I must go, for love is call - ing,

(Melody)

Min - ka, Min - ka, fair - est maid - en, Min - ka, Min - ka mine.
Call - ing me to be with Min - ka, Fair - est Min - ka mine.

Min - ka, Min - ka, fair - est maid - en, Min - ka mine.____
Call - ing me to be with Min - ka, Min - ka mine.____

When a person takes a song and adds parts or changes it in some other way, we say that he or she has **arranged** the song.

The arranger of "Minka" gave both parts a chance to sing the melody. Can you find the places in the song where the harmony part changes position?

This song is arranged so that, most of the time, the harmony moves more slowly than the melody. When you sing the melody part, use bouncy, **staccato** articulation and bright vocal color. Sing the harmony part with **legato** articulation and dark tone color.

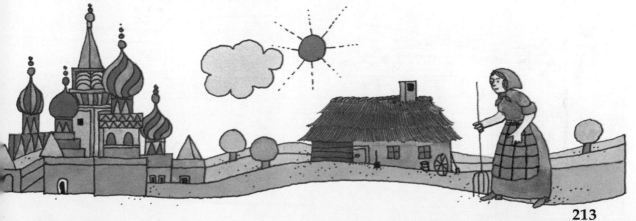

213

GREEN GROW THE LAURELS

American Folk Song

Developing good breath control can help you sing more expressively. To sing the descant for this song, prepare your breathing so that you can sing two lines in one breath. Be sure to plan your breathing at the beginning of each phrase so that you have some breath left at the end.

Change to red, white and blue.

he loves an - oth - er one bet - ter than me.
change the green lau - rels to red, white and blue.

HEY, HO! ANYBODY HOME?

English Round

How can you plan your breathing so that the end of this round connects to the beginning? HINT: The best places to breathe are at the ends of the second and third phrases.

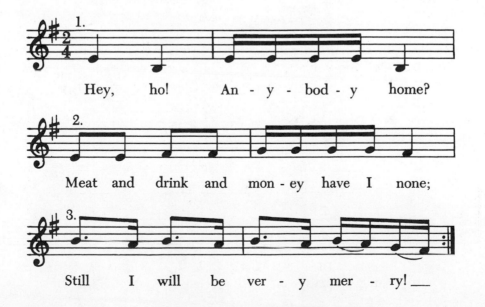

Hey, ho! An - y - bod - y home?

Meat and drink and mon - ey have I none;

Still I will be ver - y mer - ry! ___

Good **diction** is important for a clean, clear choral sound. The word **diction** refers to the way you enunciate the words in a song. The three rounds on these pages will give you a chance to practice this skill.

Begin by clearly sounding the consonants and vowels in each word. The pure vowel sounds are **ah eh ee oh oo.** Say each one. Then sing them up and down.

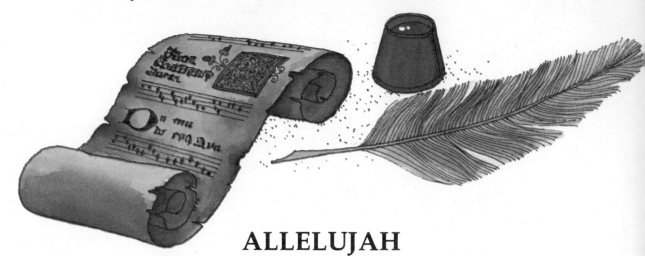

ALLELUJAH

French Canon

The words to this song are in French. Practice saying them, then singing them. Remember to use the pure vowel sounds you learned.

ah-leh-loo-yah, ah-leh-loo-yah, loo-ah^{n}zh (zh = z in "azure")
ah dee-uh ah-leh-loo-yah

Al - le - lu - jah, Al - le - lu - jah, Lou -
Al - le - lu - jah, Al - le - lu - jah, To

anges   à   Dieu____ Al - le - lu - jah.
God   sing   prais - es Al - le - lu - jah.

VIVA, VIVA LA MUSICA

Words and Music by Michael Praetorius

The Latin words "Viva la musica" mean "Long live music." Pronounce them like this: vee-vah vee-vah lah moo-zee-kah.

KYRIE

Traditional Round

The Greek words "Kyrie eleison" mean "Lord have mercy." Pronounce them like this: kih-ree-eh kih-ree-eh eh-lay-zohn.

IN BAHÍA

Words Adapted

Brazilian Folk Song

Sing "In Bahia" first in two parts, then add the third part. The third part is made up mostly of chord roots.

When you know the song, listen to the rhythms played on the recording. Learn to play each pattern. Then some may play the accompaniment while others sing.

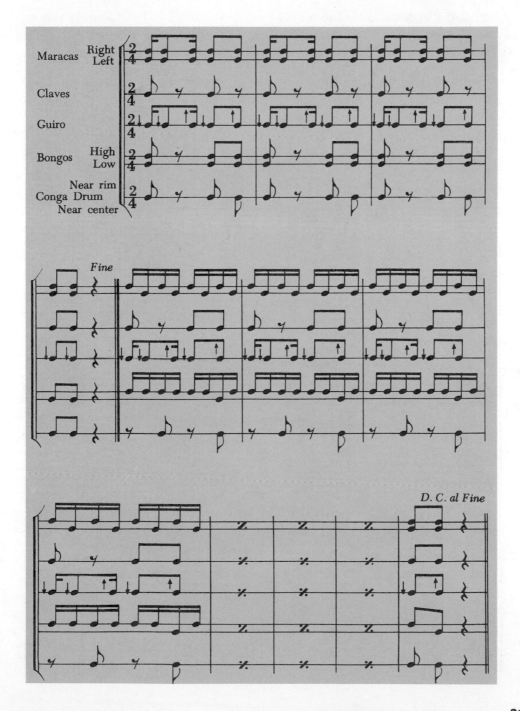

ALL CREATURES OF OUR GOD AND KING

Translated by William H. Draper
From a poem by St. Francis of Assisi

German Melody

This song gives you another good chance to practice breath control. Look at the music. Where are the best places to breathe? Sing the song. Were you right?

All crea-tures of our God and King, Lift

All crea-tures of our God and

up your voice and with us sing Al - le -

King, Lift up your voice, sing Al - le -

lu - ia! Al-le-lu - ia! Thou burn-ing sun with gold-en

lu - ia! Al-le-lu - ia! Thou

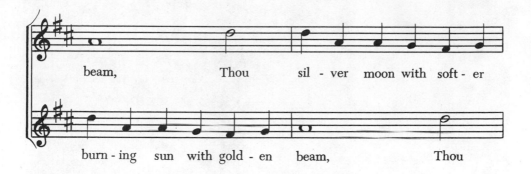

beam, Thou sil - ver moon with soft - er

burn - ing sun with gold - en beam, Thou

gleam! Al - le - lu - ia! Al - le - lu - ia! Al - le -

sil - ver moon, Al - le - lu - ia! Al - le - lu - ia! Al - le -

f

lu - ia! Al - le - lu - ia! Al - le - lu - ia!

f

lu - ia! Al - le - lu - ia! Al - le - lu - ia!

"All Creatures of Our God and King" is written in **imitation.** The harmony part imitates the melody. When you sing a round or canon you are
also singing in imitation. In a round, everyone sings the same melody. But
in the song on this page, the melodies are not always the same. Can you
find the places in the song where the imitation stops?

THANKSGIVING HYMN

Words Translated by Theodore Baker

Netherlands Folk Song
Arranged by Edward Kremser

1. We gath-er to-geth-er to ask the Lord's bless-ing,
2. Be-side us to guide us, our God with us join-ing,
3. We all do ex-tol thee, thou lead-er tri-um-phant,

He chas-tens and has-tens his will to make known;
Or-dain-ing, main-tain-ing his king-dom di-vine,
And pray that thou still our de-fend-er will be.

The wick-ed op-press-ing, now cease __ from dis-tress-ing.
So from the be-gin-ning the fight __ we were win-ning;
Let thy con-gre-ga-tion es-cape __ trib-u-la-tion.

Sing prais-es to his name; __ he for-gets not his own.
Thou, Lord, wast at our side, __ all __ glo-ry be thine.
Thy name be ev-er praised! O __ Lord, make us free!

222

Do you know what it means to sing "out of tune"? "Out of tune" is a phrase people use to describe a performance that is off pitch. The performers do not sing wrong notes, but they sing a little above or below the notes. This makes the performance sound weak and unpleasant.

You can help yourself to sing "in tune" by finding tricky sections of a song and practicing them.

For example, the descant at the bottom of the page contains some skips that might be tricky to sing in tune. Sing the patterns below. Then sing the descant on *la*. Then add the words. Choose the part that best fits the range of your voice. A few will sing the higher part, while most may sing the lower part.

La la la la la la   La la la la la la

La la la la la la

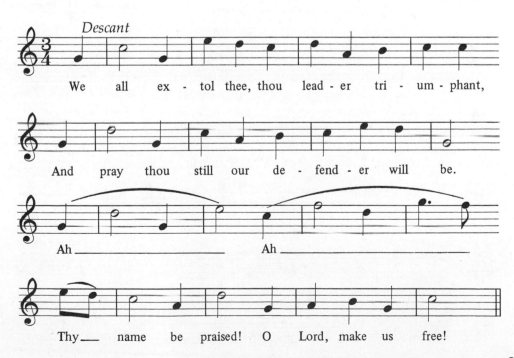

Descant

We all ex-tol thee, thou lead-er tri-um-phant,

And pray thou still our de-fend-er will be.

Ah _____   Ah _____

Thy __ name be praised! O Lord, make us free!

WALKIN' IN THE SUNSHINE

Words and Music by Roger Miller
Arranged by Fred Bock

FUM, FUM, FUM

English Words Adapted

Spanish Carol

mild,   Son of Mar - y, Vir - gin Ho - ly,   in a

Fum,   fum,   fum,

2nd Time to ⊕

sta - ble small and low - ly, Fum,   fum,   fum.

Fum,   fum,   fum, ___ Fum, fum,   fum.

On De - cem - ber five and twen - ty, Fum, fum,   fum,

On De - cem - ber five and twen - ty, Fum, fum,   fum, There was

⊕ *decresc.*   ***pp***

Fum, fum,   fum,   Fum,   fum,   fum. ___

Fum, fum,   fum,   Fum,   fum,   fum. ___

GO TELL IT ON THE MOUNTAIN

Spiritual Arranged by Buryl Red

Go, tell it on the moun-tain, O-ver the hills and

Go, tell it on the moun-tain, O-ver the hills and

ev-ery-where; Go, tell it on the

ev-ery-where; Go, tell it on the

moun-tain That Je-sus Christ is born!

moun-tain That Je-sus Christ is born!

1. While shep-herds kept their watch-ing O'er
2. The shep-herds feared and trem-bled When
3. Down in a low-ly man-ger Our

1. Shep - herds watched o'er
2. Shep - herds feared, a-
3. Low - ly man - ger

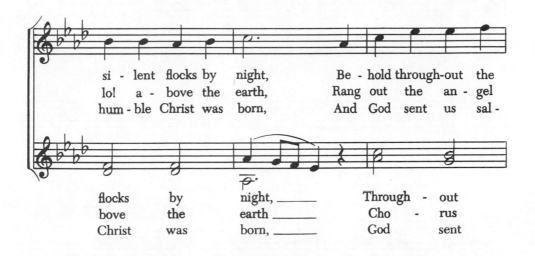

si - lent flocks by night,   Be - hold through-out the
lo! a - bove the earth,   Rang out the an - gel
hum - ble Christ was born,   And God sent us sal -

flocks   by   night, _____   Through - out
bove   the   earth _____   Cho - rus
Christ   was   born, _____   God sent

The Journey of the Magi c. 1430 by Stefano di Giovanni Sassetta (1392?-1450).
Tempera on panel.   The Metropolitan Museum of Art. Bequest of Maitland F. Griggs, 1943.

heav - ens   There shone a   ho - ly   light. _____
cho - rus   That hailed our   Sav - ior's   birth. _____
va - tion   That bless - ed   Christ - mas   morn. _____

heav - ens   shone   a _____ light. _____
hailed   the   Sav - ior's _____ birth. _____
us   that   Christ - mas _____ morn. _____

Go,   tell it on the moun - tain,   O - ver the hills and

Go,   tell it on the moun - tain,   O - ver the hills and

ev - ery - where;   Go,   tell it on the moun - tain That

ev - ery - where; _   Go, tell it on the moun - tain That

1. 2.   **3.**

Je - sus Christ is born, born, That Je - sus Christ is born!

Je - sus Christ is _ born, born, That Je - sus Christ is _ born!

ROCK OF AGES

Words by Frances Fox Sandmel, *et. al.*   Traditional Hebrew Melody

Sing this song using "la" until you can sing the skips in tune. Then add the words.

1. Rock of A - ges, God a - bove, Hear we pray our grate - ful song.
2. Kin - dling now the can - dles bright, Greet with joy each glow - ing flame.

Not our pow - er, but thy love And thy spir - it make us strong.
Ded - i - cate your life to right, Faith and free - dom to pro - claim.

Foes have cruel - ly fought us, But thy word has ev - er taught us
That men may be hear - ing: Lo, the time is near - ing

How to live; Thanks we give, Cour - age thou hast brought us.
Which will see All men free, Ty - rants dis - ap - pear - ing.

CINDY

Traditional Words

Southern Banjo Tune
Arranged by Kurt Miller

Plan your own interpretation of "Cindy." What decisions will you have to make about

breath control?   phrasing?   dynamics?

articulation?   tone color?

(detail) *Ralph Wheelock's Farm*, 1822, Francis Alexander (1800–1880, U.S.).
National Gallery of Art, Washington, D.C. Gift of Edgar William and Bernice Chrysler Garbisch.

Verse 1.

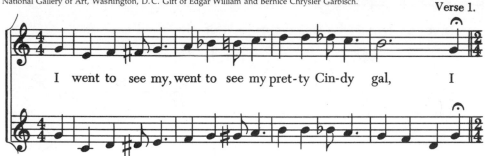

I went to see my, went to see my pret-ty Cin-dy   gal,   I

I went to see my, went to see my pret-ty Cin-dy   gal, oh, yes, I

have   no   nick - el;   have   no   dime;   I

wish I had a nick-el,   I wish I had a dime,   I

232

have no girl to love me all the time. Get a-long

wish I had a pret-ty girl to love me all the time. Please won't you

home._____ Get a-long home._____ Get a-long

go now, Cin-dy, get on home? Go now, Cin-dy, get on home!

home._____ I'll mar-ry you some-day.

Go now, Cin-dy, get on home, I'll mar-ry you some-day.

Verse 2.

I wish I had a nee-dle, as fine as I could

Loo,_____ Loo,_____

sew. I'd sew my-self to his coat-tail and

Loo,_____

down the road we'd go. Home, ____

Down the road we'd go. Get a-long home, Cin - dy, Cin - dy, get a -long

Home, ____ Home, ____

home, Cin - dy, Cin - dy; Get a - long home, Cin - dy,

____ I'll mar - ry you some - day. ____ I'll

Cin - dy, I'll mar - ry you some - day. ____ I'll

mar - ry you, I'll mar - ry you, I'll mar - ry you some -

mar - ry you, I'll mar - ry you, I'll mar - ry you some -

day, ____ Cin - dy?

day, now won't you go a - way, Cin - dy?

A NEW YEAR CAROL

Words Anonymous

Music by Benjamin Britten

1. Here we bring new wa-ter from the well so clear,
2. Sing reign of Fair Maid, with gold up-on her toe,
3. Sing reign of Fair Maid, with gold up-on her chin,

For to wor-ship God with this hap-py New Year.
O-pen you the West Door and turn the Old Year go.
O-pen you the East Door and let the New Year in.

Refrain 1., 2.

Sing le-vy dew, sing le-vy dew, the wa-ter and the wine;

The sev-en bright gold wires and the bu-gles that do shine.

3.

Sing le-vy dew, sing le-vy dew, the wa-ter and the

wine; The sev-en bright gold wires and the bu-gles that do shine.

HALELUYOH

Jewish Folk Song

After you have learned to sing "Haleluyoh," add this descant. Begin the descant on the fifth line of music.

Ha - le, ha - le - lu - yoh, Ha - le, ha - le - lu - yoh,

Ha - le, ha - le - lu - yoh, Ha - le, ha - le - lu - yoh.

LULLABY OF THE SEA

Words Anonymous

Music by
Arthur Frackenpohl

You need greater concentration to sing softly than to sing loudly. After you have learned this song, sing it loudly and fully. Then sing it softly, but with the same degree of control.

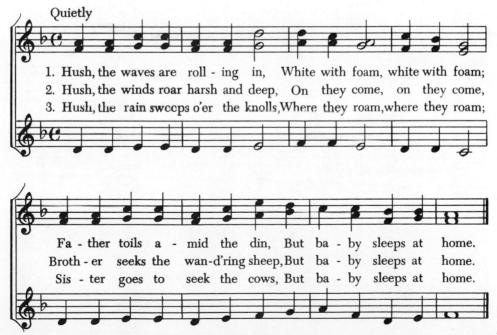

1. Hush, the waves are roll - ing in, White with foam, white with foam;
2. Hush, the winds roar harsh and deep, On they come, on they come,
3. Hush, the rain sweeps o'er the knolls, Where they roam, where they roam;

Fa - ther toils a - mid the din, But ba - by sleeps at home.
Broth - er seeks the wan-d'ring sheep, But ba - by sleeps at home.
Sis - ter goes to seek the cows, But ba - by sleeps at home.

YOU'VE GOT A FRIEND

Arranged by Buryl Red

Words and Music by Carole King

238

soon   I ____ will   be   there ____   be   there ___   To
call   my ____ name   out   loud; ___   out   loud; ___   and

soon   I ____ will   be   there ____   To
call   my ____ name   out   loud;   and

bright - en   up ___   e - ven   your   dark - est   night. _____
soon   you'll   hear ___   me ___ knock - in'   at ___ your   door. _____

You   just   call ____   my   name ___

_____   You   just   call ____   out   my ____ name ___

_____   and   know ____   wher - ev - er   I   am ___

_____   and   you   know ____   wher - ev - er   I   am ___

_____   I'll   come   run - nin', ___   run - nin', ___

_____   I'll   come   run - nin' ___

run - nin', _____ to see you a - gain.__

to see you a - gain. _____

__ Oh, __ Win - ter, spring, sum - mer or fall __

mf (Melody)

__ Oh, __ Win - ter, spring, sum - mer or fall __ All you have to

All you have to do is call _____ and I'll be__

do _____ is call _____ and I'll be __

1. and 3.
there. _____ You've got a friend._

mf

__ there. _____

3rd time through, go to Coda

You've got a friend._

You've got a friend. _____

1st time through, go back to beginning

(Melody)

You've got a friend. ___ If the sky __

240

THE POWER AND GLORY

Arranged by Buryl Red

Words and Music by Phil Ochs

Jefferson National Expansion Memorial Arch, St. Louis, Missouri, 1967, Eero Saarinen.
Hans Namuth/Photo Researchers

With enthusiasm

1. & 4. C'- mon and take a walk with me through this green and grow-in' land,
2. From Col - o - ra - do, Kan-sas, and the Car - o - li - nas, too, Vir -
3. Yet she's on - ly as rich as the poor - est of the poor,

Walk through the mead-ows and the moun-tains and the sand, Walk through the
gin - ia and A - las - ka, from the old to the new, Tex - as and O -
On - ly as free as a pad-locked pris-on door, On - ly as

val - leys and the riv - ers and the plains, Walk through the sun and
hi - o and the Cal - i - for - nia shore: Tell me, who could
strong as our love for this land, On - ly as tall as we

DOWN BY THE RIVERSIDE

Spiritual
Arranged by Buryl Red

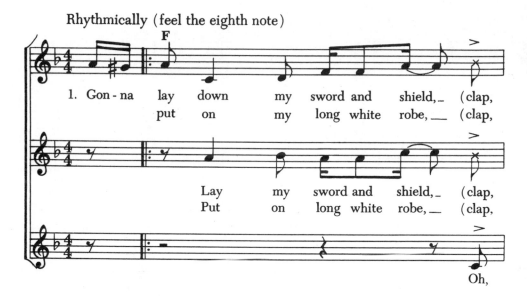

Rhythmically (feel the eighth note)

1. Gon-na lay down my sword and shield, _ (clap,
   put on my long white robe, _ (clap,

Lay my sword and shield, _ (clap,
Put on long white robe, _ (clap,

Oh,

clap) down by the riv-er-side, _ (clap,

clap) down by the riv-er-side, o _ (clap,

down, oh,

stud-y war no more, _ oh

Stud - y war no more, _

stud-y war no more, _ I ain't gon-na

stud - y war no more, _

stud-y war no more, I ain't gon-na

no more,

stud-y war no more,

stud-y war no more, _ oh,

stud - y war no more, _

CLASSIFIED INDEX

POEMS

ROUNDS AND CANONS

ALPHABETICAL INDEX